Wild Flowers

Francesca Greenoak

Macdonald Guidelines

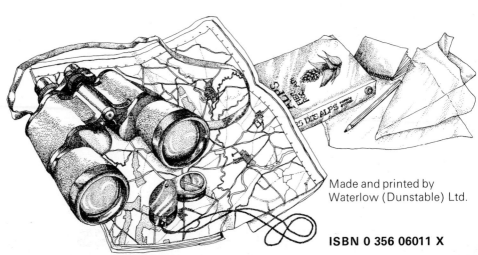

Made and printed by
Waterlow (Dunstable) Ltd.

ISBN 0 356 06011 X

Contents

© Macdonald Educational Ltd. 1977

First published 1977
Macdonald Educational Ltd.
Holywell House, Worship Street
London EC2A 2EN

Every weed a wild flower?

The vermilion brilliance of field poppies must be one of the most evocative scenes of summer. Yet if we put ourselves in the place of a farmer, that glorious colour represents economic loss. High technology is employed in the electric scanning of seed and in the formulation of weed-killers to keep cereal crops pure of weeds—and that

Bermuda buttercup

Persicaria

tended in one place, grow wild and troublesome in another situation.

Long live weeds

The Bermuda buttercup is one such plant. Despite its common name it is not a buttercup, but a member of the oxalis family, and

Fat hen

includes poppies, cornflowers and corn marigolds, as well as those plants more generally accepted as weeds, such as charlock, bindweed and wild oat.

What then is a wild flower? The definition must obviously include weeds. The dictionary describes wild flowers as 'plants which are not cultivated', but this is only half the story. Some flowers, carefully it comes from South Africa. The delicate yellow flowers and drooping leaves grace many a garden where it is planted and cared for. But it is one of a number of 'foreigners' which, taking well to a new habitat, become naturalized, growing and reproducing quite happily without any human agency. That same Bermuda buttercup is one of the most pernicious weeds of the bulb fields of the Scilly Isles.

Though we may not notice it, we are surrounded by wild flowers, many of which we overlook by dismissing them simply as weeds. Our commonest weeds are just successful wild flowers. They happen to thrive in conditions created by human beings and hold a wealth of interest for those prepared to investigate their background a little.

For many of these 'weed-wildflowers' the association with human beings is longstanding. Analysis of pollen remains from Neolithic settlements confirms the widespread distribution of fat hen and pale persicaria around these habitations. When the stomach contents of Tollund man—preserved in a Danish peat bog for 2000 years —were examined, they were found to include both these plants. They found ideal conditions for growth in the man-made forest clearings and it was believed that early man simply gathered what grew around. However, an exciting continuation of the story has recently been revealed in the discovery of stores of fat hen seed at an early stone-age settlement in France. It seems that while the male population devoted their energies to hunting, the women learned not merely to forage, but to collect and cultivate seeds—thus becoming the first European horticulturists. Nor did stone-age families fare so badly; fat hen is a delicious vegetable lightly boiled or cooked in butter. Today fat hen, redefined as a weed, is still flourishing in the wild; a living piece of social history.

▲ A beautiful wild flower and an aggressive weed, field bindweed (or cornbind) has deep-lodged roots which can penetrate to 8 metres. A new plant can grow from a small piece of root. No wonder it is also called Devil's Guts.

Keeping an open eye

One of the most exciting aspects of developing an interest in wild flowers is that there is direct access to them almost everywhere. The opportunity for personal observation and discovery is open to anybody who stops to look at a flower. It could be by a roadside or a piece of waste ground or in the woods or fields— the breakthrough occurs when one realizes that it is not only the rare plants which are interesting, and that advanced botanical knowledge is not a prerequisite for learning to appreciate wild flowers in a variety of different ways.

But the most traditional place for wild flowers is, of course, the countryside. There are sights which make a country outing into an occasion—like the azure mist of a bluebell wood, the pink sea of a heather moor, or the intimate discovery of a patch of spring primroses. The magic of these discoveries lies not just in the flowers themselves, but in the way they conjure up the spirit of the English countryside.

One of the most interesting facts to emerge from countryside surveys is that the vast majority of visitors to the country never move out of sight of their cars. It could be that even people who have travelled many miles to get there find satisfaction in simply having a wild horizon rather than the planted landscape of park and garden.

Some country flowers are old familiars: the hawthorn and gorse, the harebells and cowslips. But there are others too, nonetheless interesting for being shy. In woodland and hedgerow you only need to poke about a little to find them: dog's mercury, cow parsley, lady's bedstraw, hogweed. Appreciation of the country is increased with awareness; before long one acquires an eye for the hidden aspects of the country. There is an art to looking *for* wild flowers and an art to looking *at* them. A fascinating individuality becomes distinguishable where previously there was just an indifferent mass of green.

▼ A group negotiates a nature trail in the North of England. This particular route takes in hedgerows, woods and other familiar habitats.

▲ An artist's interpretation of a scene at the edge of a wood, showing a rich range of plant life.

In the foreground we find the purple-red flowers of red bartsia, *1*. This must be an old and undisturbed piece of land, for nearby is a rare patch of greater butterfly orchids, *2*. On the edge of the clearing is a common hedgerow plant: hedge garlic, *3*. Under the trees are quantities of a plant typical of woodland, dogs mercury, *4*, with its inconspicuous greeny flowers.

Headland, hedgerow and high street

Once you begin to look out for wild flowers it becomes apparent that they are everywhere in some shape or form. Almost every part of the countryside provides a habitat for a plant community, even places which look most unwelcoming.

Natural survivors

On high mountain slopes there are tough, sprawly little flowers such as saxifrages, hugging the ground to keep out of the cold, dry winds. Many of them can survive under snow for several years, springing to life again when there is a thaw. Some plants have developed special features—like the silvery covering of hairs of the alpine lady's mantle *(Alchemilla alpina)*, which keep the plant dry in melting snow so it can take immediate advantage of mild weather.

To come down to sea level, a shingle beach, salty and unstable, seems an unlikely site for any wild flower. But even here plants establish themselves. Spreading roots out under the shifting top layer of

▶ Red valerian, a cheerful plant of coastal regions, is as much at home on walls as on cliffs and banks. A native of central and southern Europe, it was introduced to British gardens in the sixteenth century, and it now grows wild all over Europe.

► Many hedgerows are remnants of what were once scrub and woodland. The harebells in the foreground are much more characteristic of woodland than roadside. The delicate white heads of the common hogweed are much more typical of hedgerow vegetation.

pebbles, they make use of every minute piece of humus, taking in their water from rainfall and dew.

When one considers some of the difficulties of survival raised by certain natural habitats, it seems less surprising that wild flowers invade man-made environments. Is a concrete jungle of courtyard pavings and office blocks less hospitable than a headland or cliff face? There are certainly plants which are common to both situations. Some 'free-wheelers'—such as sow thistles, curled dock and silverweed—may be found wherever there is a scrap of soil to be exploited in town or country. There are a number of plants which transfer readily from their natural habitat to a man-made one which resembles it. Red-stemmed pellitory-of-the-wall, by origin a plant of sea-cliffs, colonizes happily on old damp

walls, as does the round-leaved, greenish-yellow flowered navelwort, a rock dweller and a member of the stonecrop family.

Plants which have taken well to man-made habitats are known as *anthrophytic* species. The common names for some of these reflect their long association with people. The greater plantain, for instance, is also called the English Man's foot, owing to the fact that British explorers have inadvertently carried its seeds all over the world. The American name for rosebay willow-herb (*Epilobium angustifolium*) is fireweed, indicating its partiality for areas recently fireswept. It is now a conspicuous wasteground plant in northern Europe, having greatly increased its population since the second world war, thanks to the burned-out bomb-sites which created an ideal habitat.

Making an acquaintance

There is no better way of getting to know a wild flower than to watch it as it grows. No amount of armchair reading, however wide and detailed, will give you quite the same sense of the character of the plant. It is in this individual character that the excitement of studying wild flowers lies; the plant does not have to be a rarity to be of interest. In fact common wild flowers can be especially interesting, if one traces some of the reasons why they are so widespread.

The ideal way to investigate a flower is to start by observing the plant in its habitat. Quiz yourself, using a mixture of observation and reference to written information, to build up a fuller picture. Begin at the beginning: how did the plant begin life in the place you have found it? Are there others of the same species nearby which may have seeded it or could it be a vegetative shoot or runner from a 'parent' plant? How does it grow—big and bulky or small and delicate? What kind of bedfellows does it have and how does it hold its own against competition? What kind of flower does it boast: a bright, scented bloom to attract pollinating insects, or a tiny and insignificant one? In that case it may rely on its pollen being scattered by the wind. And what are the most likely possibilities for the dispersal of its seeds—animals, insects or the wind?

Put crudely, the main business in the life of every plant is to grow and reproduce itself in increasing numbers. A simple purpose perhaps, but it is the variety of means by which plants achieve it that makes botany such an absorbing pursuit.

A question of identity

Whether the observer is novice or expert, the question which usually springs first to

▲ Three ways of looking at a teasel: this stylized one is from the *Latin Herbarius*.

Published only a year later in 1485, the *German Herbarius* is more naturalistic.

This accomplished illustration is taken from Fuch's *De Historia Stirpium* of 1542.

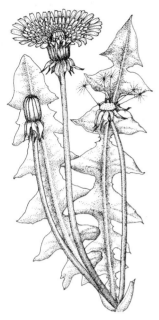

▲ **Dandelion.** This familiar plant has a flower composed of many 'ray' florets. The multiple flower is typical of the compositae family, to which the daisy-like **feverfew** also belongs. This flower has both 'ray' and 'disc' florets.

The **trifid bur marigold** has flowerheads composed entirely of 'disc' florets.

mind at the sight of a plant is 'What is it?'. There are many answers but surely '*Bellis perennis*, a member of the *Compositae* family' is no more of an answer than 'That's only a daisy'. Identification should be seen not as an end in itself but as a starting point. A name gives you a point of reference. It puts you in touch with a fund of other people's knowledge and experience which can give extra dimension to your personal focus.

Suppose you come across some daisies in a field. They are common enough flowers; you see them every day. Take another look. You may notice that certain features of the plant are variable. Where the grass is longer you will find flowerheads perched on 10 cm high stems, but where the grass is very long there will be no daisies at all.

They cannot support themselves against exuberant scrubby competition. That is why they grow so well in lawns which resemble grazed pastures, their natural habitat. In grass which is cropped short by sheep or rabbits—or cut smooth by a lawnmower—there will be flowers growing almost at ground level, the stems only a centimetre or so in length.

Daisies are ideally suited to a grassland habitat and in that kind of situation they are ubiquitous. They produce prodigious numbers of tiny seeds; it has been estimated that an acre of suitable ground might contain 11 million viable daisy seeds. But with the danger of getting a flowerhead bitten off at any moment, daisies don't just rely on seeds to proliferate. Healthy plants put out shoots which come from between

11

the leaves and the stem. From these new plants grow up, creating the familiar daisy patch.

Like all green plants, daisies rely on their leaves to make food. The way these leaves grow, in a 'rosette' pressed close to the ground, makes it difficult for teeth or mower blades to get at them effectively. They are also impervious to trampling. Indeed, trampling is actually beneficical. The tiny, dust-like seeds are picked up by the feet of animals (including human ones) and carried far afield. A sample of dust swept up from churches was found to contain a number of daisy seeds transported in this manner.

The eye of the day

There are often a number of common names for everyday plants and these speak to us descriptively or refer to old usages. The English common name 'daisy' or 'day's eye' testifies to the observational powers of a previous generation, for the daisy flower is light-sensitive, closing in the dark and opening again with the dawn.

Latin names can also be revealing. Each separate species of plant has two names in the Linnaean system which is used worldwide. The generic first name may derive from a number of sources. Examples include the names first brought into use by classical authors like Virgil or Pliny: *Quercus* (oak), *Hedera* (ivy), *Bellis* (daisy), or names commemorating famous botanists, such as *Fuschia* (Fuchs, the 16th century physician and herbalist) and *Linnea* (Linneaus, the famous natural historian who brought the two-name system into common usage). Yet other derivations are geographical, as in *Lobivia*—an anagram of Bolivia, where this species of cactus is found.

The second name is generally descriptive, and shows a similar variety of form.

Foetidus (stinking), or *davidii* (in honour of the nineteenth century missionary and plant collector), are cases in point. All the plant species are grouped together into families; that is, groups of plants which share significant characteristics. Thus we have the crucifers (*Cruciferae*), a large family of flowers with four petals arranged in a cross formation; the bellflowers (*Campanulaceae*); the iris family (*Iridaceae*) and so on.

To return to the daisy, *bellis perennis*: the "bellis" has two interpretations. Some say

▲ This grass of Parnassus acts as a sun reflector to basking insects. They find the temperature of the white and yellow cup-shaped flowers of spring warmer than that of the surrounding air.

that aptly for so beautiful a flower, the name comes from the latin adjective meaning pretty. Another school holds that the Latin for 'war' was the origin, referring to the use of a daisy poultice to assuage pain and bruising. (Bruisewort is another common name).

Perennis, the second part of the name, indicates that the plant is perennial. The upper parts of the plant die back in winter but tiny buds lie dormant, protected by the surface soil and the dead parts of the plant until milder weather comes.

A close inspection of a daisy flower confirms that it is in fact, not a single flower but a composite of tiny tubular florets—white outer ones and inner yellow ones. This places it in the family *Compositae* which includes all such multiple flowers—among them thistles and dandelions. It is salutary to note that while botanists know a very great deal about plants, particularly the flora of the western world which has been studied over thousands of years, there

▲ This plant monster of damp places is giant hogweed, a magnificent representative of the umbellifer family. Surely a feast for insects!

are basic questions to which even the most erudite botanists have no explanation. Anyone who ever made a daisy chain will .have noticed the tiny hairs softly clothing the stem. The overall hairiness of daisy plants varies considerably though nobody has yet been able to pin down why this is so. But does this impair our primary response to the beauty of the plant? The real nature of plants is not reducible to a list of facts. There is no reason why one flower is different from another any more than there is a reason for different species of birds. We can only look at our wild flowers and plot the intricate relationships with other forms of life. There are thousands of variations; diversity is a delight, not a problem demanding an ultimate answer.

The cycle of life

It is obvious to even the most casual observer that different seasons bring forth different scenes of wild flowers. Before the first glimmerings of spring, the snowdrops and the celandines make their appearance, and as the weather becomes milder and the days lengthen, first one species then another dominates the floral landscape.

Food factories

Green plants have the ability to photosynthesise; they don't take in ready-made foods, but actually build up nutrient from air and water. This process can only take place in the presence of sunlight. The basic necessities of life for a wild flower—light, space and adequate supply of water—are at a premium in a plant-crowded environment. Every year each plant needs to expose enough leaves to the light to build up the considerable resources necessary to produce flowers and seeds or, if it does not flower that year, to maintain and increase itself ready for the time when it will.

An evergreen plant like ivy, with tough leaves that survive throughout the winter, can make food throughout the year. However it is noticeable that ivy which climbs on walls or on cliffs grows faster than that in the woods, where the heavy shade cast by trees allows two bursts of growth in spring and autumn. Ivy leaves grow densely, angled to catch the maximum light and forming a cover beneath which nothing else can grow. But in fields, hedgerows and on waste ground, many plants co-exist side by side, but they have their main periods of growth at different times during the year.

If you watch a piece of damp roadside you might find that early in the year the pioneer celandines will first show their glossy green leaves, then the shining yellow of their flowers. Just a little later the taller leaves of the cow parsley appear, followed by the flat flowerheads, giving the whole area the aspect of being decorated with white lace. The trees and shrubs—ash elder and hawthorn—put out their leaves and flowers later on, and at ground level, poppies and the cow parsley's stouter relative, the hogweed, appear towards the height of the summer. With the longer days of autumn the *Chenopodia* take over—the fat hen, goosefoots and oraches.

In a deciduous wood, the spring holds the greatest variety of ground flora. Primroses, wood anemones and dog's mercury appear in quick relays and bluebells take advantage of the light, sunny conditions

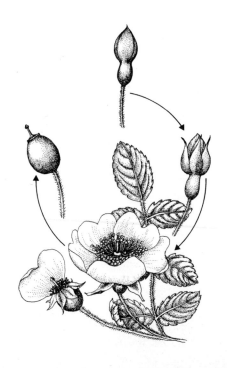

before tree leaves form a canopy which shades the ground.

An imposed order

Habitats such as hedgerows are artificially maintained by hedge cutting and mowing. Similarly grasslands are reaped for hay and grazed by animals. But without any outside interference in reasonably fertile, temperate conditions, the whole aspect of these environments would change over a period of years. The small, low-growing plants would gradually be shaded out by the larger and stronger shrubs, which would themselves give way eventually to trees. Indeed it is probably true to suppose that if human interference were removed, the greater part of northern Europe and north America would return to forest wilderness.

▲ The life cycle of the common ragwort may be repeated several times in the course of a single year, an average plant producing over 50,000 seeds. Ragwort is also capable of reproducing vegetatively by means of root buds.

▶ The honeysuckle flower guards against self-pollination; its male and female parts mature in turn. Several seeds are contained in each red berry.

◀ From rosebud to rosehip. The fragrant white blooms of the field rose are pollinated by flying beetles. Note how in this species the styles (female parts) are joined together to form a single column.

The calendar in bloom

Over the centuries, many of our wild flowers have acquired a public significance, often linked with seasonal changes or festival times. While times change and many superstitions and religious beliefs have lost most of their meaning for us, the old sayings continue to be repeated. They have become part of our consciousness of the seasons.

There is the holly and the ivy and the mistletoe of Christmas, the Easter primroses and cowslips, and at Palm Sunday, the sense that Spring has truly arrived with the catkins and pussy willow. Even in these days of central heating we still remember the springtime weather lore: 'Ne'er cast a clout till may be out', and

> The oak before the ash
> And we shall have a splash.
> The ash before the oak
> And we shall have a soak.

In high summer children still make daisy chains and plantain catapaults, and there is the adage that summer has really arrived when you can cover seven daisies in a single tread. Autumn brings conkers and the hips and haws—a heavy crop of which is said, inaccurately, to presage a bitter winter.

Most people who take more than a passing interest in plants have their own special favourites; flowers with an established personal intimacy which serve as landmarks of one's own private natural year. Opposite is an idiosyncratic calendar: gorse is not at its best in November, but in a month when very little blooms, I am glad to see the yellow flowers, recalling the old saying: 'When gorse is out of bloom then kissing is out of season.'

JANUARY

Hazel catkins

APRIL

Cow or hedge parsley

JULY

Teasel

OCTOBER

Spindle berry

FEBRUARY

Coltsfoot

MARCH

Sweet violet

MAY

Hawthorn

JUNE

Red clover

AUGUST

Marsh mallow

SEPTEMBER

Parasol mushroom

NOVEMBER

Gorse

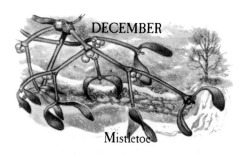

DECEMBER

Mistletoe

Everything in its place

Plants tend to grow in generally recognisable communities. We can speak in broad terms of the flowers of the chalk, and of limestone, of mountain, bog and coastal flora. But things aren't really as neat as these categories would imply. Plants are forever upsetting our mental filing system by turning up in the most unlikely spots. Who would think of looking for Mediterranean mountain plants along a Gloucester dockside? Yet there they blow. A number of seeds were probably brought in with a load of granite chippings; they grew and put forth a splendid show of flowers, despite completely alien conditions.

Some plants are so reliably specific to one kind of habitat that they are known as 'indicator' plants. You can be pretty sure you are standing on basic rock where you find the little saxifrage *Saxifraga oppositifolia*, whereas its relative *Saxifraga stellaris* is a plant of acid rock.

Climate as well as soil type has considerable influence on the vegetation of a particular area. There are many factors which help determine habitat: soil, temperature, wind, light and humidity among them. Often one errs in trying to pinpoint a single dominant influence, since there are infinite variations. The primrose, for instance, has been observed to shun poor soils in relatively dry areas, but where rainfall is high it grows in a number of sites regardless of soil composition.

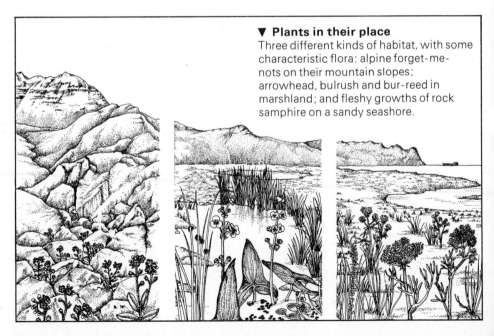

▼ **Plants in their place**
Three different kinds of habitat, with some characteristic flora: alpine forget-me-nots on their mountain slopes; arrowhead, bulrush and bur-reed in marshland; and fleshy growths of rock samphire on a sandy seashore.

▲ Trees in exposed positions grow small and slowly. This ancient wood in Dartmoor is severely predated by the winter moth.

▼ Two similar-looking bedstraws—but limestone bedstraw loves lime, and heath bedstraw hates it.

Salty seed beds

One type of vegetation more obviously linked to a single geographic factor is that of the seacoast. Most maritime species do not grow naturally away from the sea. But even here there are exceptions. It was recently recorded that sea aster, sea plantain and annual seablite were flourishing on several inland roadsides. A strange phenomenon—but not so unaccountable when it is remembered that these roads are de-iced in winter by large quantities of rock salt. Extensive though our knowledge of the soil and climatic preferences of plants is, they still have surprises, even for the most expert.

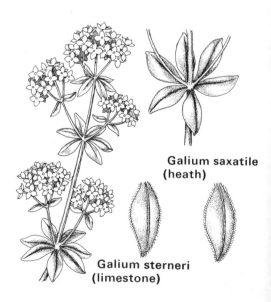

Galium saxatile (heath)

Galium sterneri (limestone)

Woodland wild flowers

No longer are Europe and much of North America covered by thick natural woodland. Vast portions of forest have been cleared by man over the ages, but what remains, with the woods that have been planted, provide rich habitats for a great number of plant and animal species.

Even the smallest, artificial plantation makes a plant habitat. Of all plant communities, woodland is perhaps the most complex. There are four identifiable layers of vegetation: ground plants, such as mosses; a 'field' layer; shrubs, and trees. On different soils in different geographic areas different kinds of plant life will be found in each layer.

▲ Ash is one of those trees which can self-seed itself in hedgerow, field or garden as well as in woodland. The flowers are part insect, part wind-pollinated.

▲ Foxglove, typically a plant of woodland clearings, may also be found in a variety of other habitats, including scrubland, heaths and mountains.

▲ Herb Bennet, the blessed plant which keeps away evil, is another woodland flower which has acclimatized to hedgerows and waysides, where there is damp and shade.

Woodlands only

▲ Townhall clock. This aptly named little woodland plant is so inconspicuous with its tiny green flowerheads, that it seems to be rarer than it is.

Some woodland plants, such as those pictured opposite, are hardy and do not demand a specialized kind of habitat. These can thrive not only in woodland but in the hedgerows, and by roadsides too. Other plants—like those on this page—are naturally suited to the sheltered damp confines of woodland and rarely grow naturally elsewhere.

It is fascinating to note that though members of completely unrelated families, the bluebell and the anemone show similarities in their pattern of growth. Both send up shoots and leaves early in spring and produce a profuse display of flowers which can dominate the woodland scene for a short period. They then disappear completely from view until the next year. They make maximum use of the light season, then 'go underground'; the anemone storing its food in underground stems, the bluebell in its bulb.

▲ Wood anemone. Its elegant blooms grace the woods early in the year. The sight of the flowers tossing in the cold spring winds earned the name 'windflower'.

▲ Bluebell. Perhaps the best-loved flower of English oakwoods. Its flowering life is splendid but brief, all over by early June. The seed pods ripen soon after.

The forest backdrop

Most woodlands, natural and planted, are dominated by one or two types of tree species; oak, beech, ash, or conifers, such as larch, pines or firs. There are certain flowers which are associated with particular types of woodland, and are rarely, if ever, found elsewhere. There has been some anxiety over the past few decades among conservationists over the intensive planting of conifer forest at the expense of broadleaf trees, since they tend to harbour a smaller variety of plants in the field layer. However, recent research encouragingly reveals that there is a richer selection of wildlife in these plantations than was originally supposed.

Natural pine forest clothes much of central Europe, Scandinavia and North America. But Northwest Europe tends to a climax woodland of oak rather than pine, except in highland regions. Wetland gives rise to alders and willows. In chalky soils beech may be dominant, and ash is a tree which favours limestone.

The flora of woodlands

The richness of the field layer of flora is linked closely with the amount of light which is available. In dense dark conifer woods, plants have to be shade-tolerant to survive. By contrast, the wild flowers of an oakwood have a much easier time. Unlike the needles of conifers, oakleaves decompose quickly providing good humus. There is comparatively greater light in an oak forest—even in the height of summer—so that while the main glory of an oakwood is in the spring, you can find flowers such as Herb Robert and enchanter's nightshade flowering in the summer months. Ashwoods, too, allow in light and boast a rich flora—including columbines and ramsons (wild garlic).

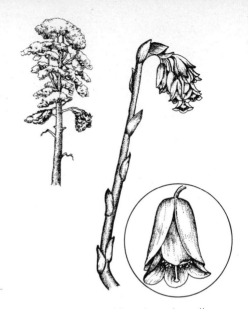

▲ This curious-looking plant, the yellow birdsnest, is parasitic on the roots of pine. It has no chlorophyll of its own and therefore has no green leaves.

But in beechwoods, flowers have to make the most of the early spring days. For the leaves, once out, form an impenetrable canopy through which very little light can filter. In the gloom of a beechwood summer, the field layer is almost absent except for the pale beauty of helleborines and a few other plants which positively enjoy damp and shade.

In mild conditions you find birch growing among the dominant forest trees, but when the going gets tough, up on the treeline of mountains and in the cold northern regions, the birch comes into its own. Birchwoods are not renowned for the richness of their field layer. Not many plants can stand the cold or the nitrogen-deficient soils, and flowers which do get a foothold are usually grazed by hungry animals. Fungi are the main glory of birchwood. Some magnificent specimens can be seen, such as the ravishing fly agaric with its

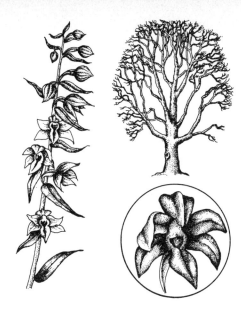

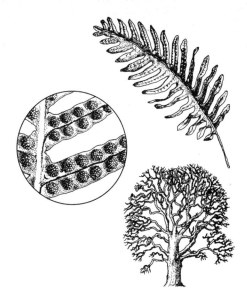

▲ The fragrant dark-red helleborine is a rare plant, found deep in beechwoods, on limestone soils. It has a number of cousins who also share its habitat.

▲ The polypody fern is often found on sloping boughs of oak trees. Its underground stems run along the fissures in the bark, picking up the rich humus there.

spotted red cap.

Bluebell behavior

Investigation into the effects of large numbers of people to forest areas has shown up some dramatic consequences for bluebells. It is evident that they, more than most flowers, suffer very badly from the tramp of feet in the early part of the year. In heavily trodden places, the next year's plants consisted of extremely weak and scrawny specimens. Even picking the flowers—whether done by taking the whole flower stalk or nipping the stalk off just above ground level—seems not to have such a bad effect. The bulbs are unable to lay in a store of food because, without their leaves, they are unable to photosynthesize. Whereas continued picking would severely weaken the plant over a period of time, foot traffic has an almost immediate effect.

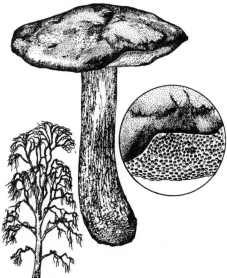

▲ The boletus scaber is another example of a fungus which lives in mycorrhizal relationship with tree roots. This boletus feeds from the roots of birch.

Flowers of the field

Meadow flowers are—of all plants—the wild flowers of summer. They call to mind warm summer days, the sweet smell of grass and splashes of colour—buttercup yellow, poppy red, the blue of the meadow cranesbill—against a background of green. Such scenes must surely rate among the most pleasing and beautiful of country impressions.

A man-made habitat

Most meadows are not natural habitats in the precise sense, although some are of great antiquity, dating back 4000 years to Neolithic times when the forests were first cleared. If left to themselves without inter-ference, a grassfield will, as an experiment begun last century proves, grow into scrub and ultimately woodland. However, farmers need meadows as pasture or to be mown for hay, and regular grazing and mowing maintains a standard of arable openness.

It is not strictly true to say that the dominant plant of meadows is "grass". To make such a casual definition is to dismiss *en masse* the members of that often over-looked family *Graminaceae* (grasses). Turn a discerning eye on that mass of green stems. You will probably find five or more different grass species in any one meadow. Some of these will be commonly found growing elsewhere, but a few, such as Italian ryegrass and timothy, are specially planted by farmers for their high nutritional value.

Sometimes a selection of clover is sown with the grass seed in a meadow. But clover will usually find its way there naturally in any case, as do the other wild flowers—buttercups, plantains, vetches, poppies,

◀ A path threads through a beautiful field of the kind beloved by the impressionists. But for some, its associations are more bitter:
In Flander's fields the poppies grow, between the crosses row on row . . .

▶ A summer glory of buttercups carpets a meadow in Oxfordshire.

ragwort, thistles and Shakespeare's famous lady's smocks.

If a meadow is not ploughed and resown for several years, some of the planted species will disappear in competition with the natural flora. Some of the flowers—buttercup and ragwort for instance—are poisonous to animals and are usually avoided by them; but others like dandelion and ribgrass contain trace minerals and are beneficial to livestock. Not a great deal is known about these trace minerals, but it is now thought that the practice of putting race horses out to graze on pastures to bring them into peak condition could be scientifically justified. Some farmers consider it better practice to tolerate certain 'weed-wild flowers' in their meadows rather than to eliminate them.

▲ "But Ferdinand just liked to smell the flowers". Lazlo's classic children's hero, *Ferdinand the Bull*, was a lover of field flowers. In fact, cattle grazing is one of the best means of managing orchid meadows.

The two-tier system

In meadows and pastures—even those cropped short as an ideal lawn—there are two clear layers of vegetation. The ground layer consists of grasses and plants such as daisies and plantains which have 'rosettes' of leaves growing close-pressed to the ground. The obvious advantages of this form of growth have been mentioned earlier: the food-supply is kept safe from blades, reapers and other factors which threaten photosynthesising leaves. Many field plants can reproduce vegetatively, putting out new plants from root or stem stalk and this too enables them to thrive under pasture conditions.

The second layer of vegetation in a pasture consists of taller plants not eaten by animals, which explains why we get out-crops of ragwort and thistles towering over an otherwise flat field. Hay meadows – or those which are grazed late in the season – hold a greater abundance of wild flowers because a variety of species, including those palatable to beasts, have the opportunity to grow, flower and seed before they are subjected to any outside interference. These are marvellous places for wild flower foraging, where you can find one of the most splendid members of the buttercup family, the marsh marigold, numerous vetches and the delicate pink of the lady's smocks. If the field is somewhat chalky there will be an even greater variety of plants including the purple headed scabiouses, and the sweet-smelling wild carrot and salad burnet whose leaves are cucumber-scented. In some permanent meadowland which is not regularly ploughed and resown, there may also be orchids such as the fragrant orchid or pyramidal orchid.

By contrast the wild flowers of arable land are those which can thrive despite a large degree of disturbance. Some quick-

growing annuals such as chickweed, groundsel and ragwort can go through several generations in a single year. Nowadays most of the arable ground wild flowers will be found on the margins of fields, banished from the field proper by efficient seed 'screening' which eliminates all but the crop seed and by selective herbicides. Two common and colourful cornfield plants which have almost disappeared are corncockle and cornflower. Happily though, poppies and charlock still colour the fieldsides red and yellow and a sharp eye will usually detect the glint of the tiny scarlet pimpernel.

Detectives in the fields

There is some interesting basic sleuthing that is easy to carry out when you are investigating an area of grassland. If the landscape consists almost entirely of the

▲ A plant-by-plant survey being made, charting every individual daisy which falls within the outline of the quadrat.

common meadow grasses—with a sprinkling of clover, lucerne, or sainfoin—then you are most likely to be in a recently sown 'ley'. Older meadows not recently sown will have a larger proportion of weed-wild flowers'. In those fields which are grazed, these plants will form characteristic islands; ragwort and thistle make particularly noticeable tall clumps in comparison with the cropped turf which surrounds them. Water meadows are usually cultivated exclusively for pasture. They are very carefully maintained and flooded regularly to produce a selection of luscious flowers and grasses—a treat for the eye as well as for gourmet cattle. Generally speaking the more varied and rich the wild flower species, the older the meadow.

Heath and moor

Were one to place a sprig of heather between a marsh marigold and a bee orchid, it would not be the heather which caught the eye. It must be seen in its natural surroundings, growing in quantity. The long horizons of heath and moorland, brushing the landscape with muted purple in the summer and burnishing it rich golden-brown in the autumn, are uniquely spectacular. It is a marvellously integrated scene with plants and place in intimate relationship.

A moorland carpet

The heather species are rugged plants, adapted to extreme environmental conditions. They grow in exposed areas on poor, acid soils, such as those of high moorland and sandy lowland heaths. In what a lay person would call heather or ling, a botanist recognises a number of species. Although at a distance, they look fairly similar, it is quite easy to distinguish three of the more common 'heather' species from each other.

Calluna heather (*Calluna vulgaris*), found mostly in upland areas with a high rainfall, has a wide geographical range; from the western Mediterranean up into the Arctic. Bell heather (*Erica cinerea*), confined in distribution to western Europe, prefers drier moorland conditions, while cross-leaved heath (*Erica tetralix*) favours wet heathland. It is however, not unusual to find all three of these species growing on a single moor or heath, reflecting very local differences in environment. The wettest bogland may merge into drier and even somewhat parched areas within a short distance.

Heathland cousins

There is a greater variety of vegetation to be found on heath and moorland than at

► Three common kinds of heather. *1.* Bell Heather: leaves in whorls of three, bell-like flowers. *2.* Cross-leaved heath: leaves, as you would expect, in fours. *3.* Calluna heather: note flower spikes and leaves in neat opposite rows.

▼ Gorse, the glorious vanilla-scented bush of commons and heaths. The prickly spines are modified leaves; this shape protects the plant and reduces water loss.

first appears. There are relatives of heather: bilberry, cranberry and crowberry, several kinds of orchid, including the beautiful butterfly orchid, and, always a thrill to discover, the snowy delicate blooms of grass of Parnassus.

Heath and moorland soils are lacking in minerals; they are also deficient in nitrogen. The most successful plants of such areas are those which have special ways of dealing with these unpropitious conditions. The roots of heather species, for instance, live in close association with certain fungi which can 'fix' the nitrogen in the air. This *mycorrhizal* companionship gives the heather species a ready supply of necessary nitrogen.

Gorse is another widespread plant, of which at least four kinds are found on heath and moor. The various species bloom at different times. Like peas and other leguminous plants, gorses have lumpy 'nodules' on their roots. These contain nitrogen-fixing bacteria which ensure the plant its supply. An interesting variation on the theme occurs in other moorland plants such as the sundews and butter-

▼ Lucky white heather: scenes such as this are less common than in Victorian times, but it is still considered unlucky to refuse to buy such gypsy wares. The white-flowered variant may be found in both bell heather and in cross-leaved heath.

worts, which trap and consume insects in their leaves as a means of obtaining their nitrogen.

Threats to survival

Heathland in populated areas is a matter of concern for conservationists. Much of it is disappearing as a direct result of human activity; the encroachment of housing and agriculture and the proliferation of drainage schemes. Heaths are also taken over for use as conifer plantations.

Another hazard, particularly of dry summers, is fire. This is responsible for widespread destruction of wildlife, plants and animals. The vegetation can recover fairly quickly from small fires, but the re-colonizing plantlife is generally less diverse than the original cover. Mosses, lichen and bracken invade the scorched land, and heather and gorse, which are deep-rooted, rapidly grow again. Many of the smaller shallow-rooted plants are, however, completely burned out. A far worse situation results when small fires develop into raging and persistent infernos which may continue over several days. Even gorse and heather are scorched right down to the roots and the land, sterile and open to erosion, takes years to recolonise.

▶ Heathland 'podsol'. The dark layer in this diagram represents a barrier about 50cm down of 'hard pan', which consists of washed-down humus and minerals. This is why heathland shrubs are almost exclusively shallow-rooting plants such as heather and cowberry. Scotch pine is about the only tree which can penetrate this layer.

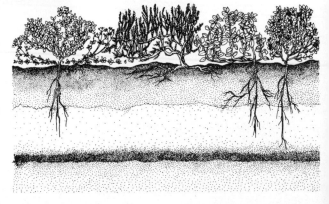

Heathland literally buzzes with activity; the abundant nectar of the heather supports several kinds of bees and wasps. Grasshoppers and crickets too find the heath environment congenial. Common lizards and adders can be disturbed sunning themselves on leaf or bracken litter. The emperor moth looks spectacular when viewed in isolation, but it blends perfectly into the landscape of the heath.

It is an open environment so camouflage is an important factor. Kestrels from neighbouring farmland may hunt over heaths while weasels prey at ground level. Rabbits—being burrowing creatures —suffer less from the open nature of the habitat, and they have a good food supply in heather and grasses. Birds such as stonechats find cover in the gorse bushes.

Grass signals

It is possible to judge the local soil and climatic conditions from an observation of the kinds of grasses which grow on heath or moorland. A sandy soil favours wavy hair grass or purple moor grass growing in clumpy tussocks, as a compliment to the dominant calluna heather. On a clay soil, purple moor grass will be the dominant plant—especially on wet sloping hillsides. In thoroughly waterlogged, boggy, acid soils may be found an expanse of unbroken 'cotton grass'—a misnomer because it is not a grass at all but a sedge with beautiful, silvery, dense flowerheads. A signifier of drier conditions than are usually found in moorland is a heavy growth of mat grass. This grass has thin spikey leaves which, in order to conserve every droplet of their water, roll themselves up tightly.

Marsh and wetlands

Rich soil, plenty of light, unlimited water—and a lush profusion of wild flowers. Everywhere you look there seems to be some form of plantlife; in the water, at the margin, up the banks and in the damp surrounding land. From early spring to late summer, this populous scene surges with life and continuously permutating colours and scents.

In many marshy places and fenland the growth is so rapid that if it were not kept in check by reed and sedge cutting, by grazing and osier cropping, willow and alder would soon take over. In a few years a mature deciduous community would shade out all the plants of open wetland. As the plants of the water edge—the sedges and reeds—die back, the dead vegetation forms a mud or peat base in which trees can get a roothold. Gradually the whole plant colony inches its way forward, reducing the water area, turning it to marshy ground and ultimately into firm soil, unless strenuous efforts are made to keep the defined margins.

Marsh vs. bog

There is a striking difference between a marsh or fen and the bogs of heath and moorland. In the latter, the peat and water is strongly acid. Fen too is peaty, but it is alkaline in nature. Marsh—simply defined as a muddy rather than peaty wetland—can be neutral to alkaline. In effect this means that heather species and other plants of poor soils are absent from marsh and fen, while the more numerous species which flourish on chalk and lime or in neutral surroundings are present in abundance.

▶ One of the most striking things about wetlands is the sheer abundance of the wildflower population. In this picture yellow rattle and red campion jostle with other flowers.

▼ This evocative picture of reed cutting in Norfolk was taken by the pioneer Victorian photographer Emerson.

There are many ecological variables on wetland, depending on the soil composition and the way it is managed, but one of the most agreeable features for the wild flower seeker is that some of the commonest flowers are among the most beautiful.

Common fenland flowers

In early summer one looks for the water violet, an aquatic relation of the primrose. Its feathery leaves grow underwater but the yellow-throated, lilac blooms rise out of the water on slender stems. Further out, the water may be paved with water-lilies. Although the leaves and the lily flowers float on top of the water, the stems stretch down to root in the pond bed, maybe 3 metres or more below the water surface.

The peppermint odour of water mint will assail you before you actually see the plant, which often clumps itself along the water margin. Here too will be the tall elegant stems of the yellow flag, a lovely wild member of the iris family. Its seeds, like those of many water plants, float on the water, to root in new muddy sites. A step or two back, overtopping the rest of the damp undergrowth, you may find impressive groups of hemp agrimony topped with soft pink flowerheads, full of nectar and beloved of insects. Their leaves resemble those of hemp—hence the name—but it is, in fact, no relation to true cannabis.

The human factor

Many water-loying plants are found not only by the traditional waterways, but in recently created man-made habitats—drainage ditches, canals, reservoirs and

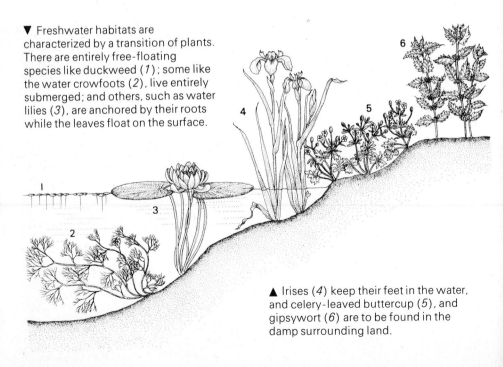

▼ Freshwater habitats are characterized by a transition of plants. There are entirely free-floating species like duckweed (1); some like the water crowfoots (2), live entirely submerged; and others, such as water lilies (3), are anchored by their roots while the leaves float on the surface.

▲ Irises (4) keep their feet in the water, and celery-leaved buttercup (5), and gipsywort (6) are to be found in the damp surrounding land.

◀ The destiny of some of the reeds on the previous page? The common reed (*Phragmites*) makes superb thatching material, though unfortunately there is less call for thatch nowadays and many reed beds are falling into disuse.

▼ The flowering rush is not, strictly speaking, a rush at all. But before it comes into flower it strongly resembles one, with its long, thin three-cornered leaves.

gravel pits. Modern drainage methods are destroying many old fens and some rare plants, such as fen ragwort, have taken refuge in damp ditches. Other waterside plants are more plentifully distributed, co-existing in sites of human activity. These include traditional European marsh species such as gipsywort and skullcap, and some interesting recent invaders' such as Himalayan balsam and the North American, orange balsam.

In some cases the rapid increase of invaders has become a problem. The drainage ditches and canals of the southern United States are clogged with the lovely blue flowers of *Eichhornis creassipis*, or water hyacinth, whose lateral shoots can connect plants hundreds of square metres apart. Introduced into the Nile River in 1957 as a "decorative species", it spread along 620 miles (1000 km) of river within the year. A thing of beauty has become a pest.

Coastal Paths

When you're having a picnic on the sheltered side of a sand-dune, the only thing you're likely to notice about the grass is that it can be very prickly. And when the wind blows sand into your sandwiches, you pack up and move to another spot. Unfortunately a few innocent picnics like this can lead to the destruction of the dune. Those holes you grubbed out to keep the Thermos and milk bottle upright, that steep slope where the children were playing avalanches; the wind which peppered your food with sand will worry at such small crannies, tearing at them until great breaches appear and the dune begins to collapse.

Guardian grasses

It is the uncomfortable grasses we have to thank for the existence of stable dunes. There are several sea-shore grasses which can colonize bare sand. They form deep, wide-ranging root systems in order to pick up the moisture which seeps quickly through the sand. They also send out underground stems (rhisomes), which increase the spread of the plant colony. These underground networks bind the sand together, and when the wind blows, the flow of sand is impeded by the grasses, causing a hump which gradually builds into a dune. Such a pile of sand would smother most plants but some sea-grasses —marram grass in particular—have the

▼ A sea pink or thrift makes its salty home among scurvy grass and bright orange lichen in a cliffside niche.

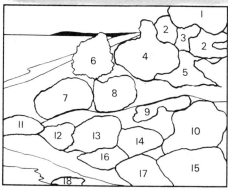

1 Sea buckthorn	**10** Viper's bugloss
2 Wild wallflower	**11** Sand cat's-tail
3 Common ragwort	**12** Sea sandwort
4 Burnet rose	**13** Sea rocket
5 Wild thyme	**14** Sand couch
6 Marram grass	**15** Valerian
7 Yellow-horned poppy	**16** Sea mayweed
8 Lyme grass	**17** Sea kale
9 Sea bindweed	**18** Kelp

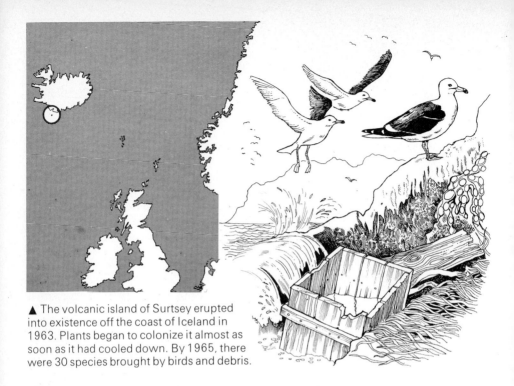

▲ The volcanic island of Surtsey erupted into existence off the coast of Iceland in 1963. Plants began to colonize it almost as soon as it had cooled down. By 1965, there were 30 species brought by birds and debris.

ability to make quick upward thrusts and rise up above the new level of sand. Marram grass can turn shifting sands into a stable environment in which other vegetation can take root.

Flowering dunes

One plant very much at home on dunes is sea sandwort. This also has spreading roots and contributes to dune stabilization. It is a low plant, its small yellow blooms couched in amongst succulent fleshy leaves. This form of leaf is common in maritime species; it acts as a water store for times of drought. Wild carrot is also found on recently formed dunes. Like marram grass, this attractive umbellifer enjoys the lime in the sand, supplied by ground-up pieces of seashell. Its stay is a temporary one though, for the lime is soon washed out by the rain.

Many of the plants of the upper seashore are scrubby annuals, well known to city botanizers. Plants such as the oraches (relatives of fat hen), can make their home in relatively poor soils, wherever the surrounding vegetation is not so strong as to out-compete them.

A most interesting feature of well-established dunes which are left undisturbed is the fertile little valleys known as 'slacks', which form on the lee side of the dunes. Humus made by the dune vegetation is washed down into the hollows, and builds up, creating a damp peaty habitat in which a delightful selection of flowers can flourish. Exploring these confined places you may be fortunate enough to find several kinds of orchid, gentians of deep stunning blue, and the starry pink blooms of narrow-leaved centaury.

Salt marsh

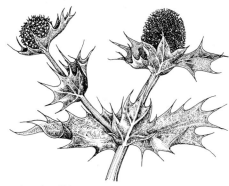

▲ A splendid plant of sand and shingle by the sea, sea holly is an unusual umbellifer.

▲ The ubiquitous curled dock may be found on arable and grassland as well as beaches.

▲ The purple-flowered sea pea does not climb but nestles into the sand or shingle.

The expansive mud flats of salt marshes are fascinating places, a kind of halfway land between sea and shoreland. The mixture of sea and river water produces a brackish environment with a variable salinity, somewhere between that of river and sea.

At the edge of the salt marsh where the tide covers the mud twice a day, the mud is very mobile and salinity at low tide is higher than that of the sea itself. In this zone the vegetation is exclusively marine. Zostera grass, beloved of brent geese, grows in the sea itself. Just above the zostera, the salicornia—or marsh samphire —takes over, its early shoots protruding through the mud like translucent green worms. Lightly boiled and buttered, this plant is served in Norfolk and Suffolk as 'poor man's asparagus'.

As summer progresses the blue-green vegetation of the higher reaches of the salt marsh begins to come into bloom. Not far from the samphire, sea aster will usually make its home. This plant, like a small Michaelmas daisy, is a favourite with one of the most beautiful of the duck species, the elegant peach-and-grey teal. Further inshore again, are the blue-mauve drifts of sea-lavender and sea purslane, interspersed with the pink of thrift (sea pink). There are a number of interesting grasses to look out for too, including the delicate red fescue grass, sea poa and townsend's cord grass— the last a relatively new colonizer.

The plants of salt marshes are specially adapted to live in saline conditions. They maintain a very high pressure of cell sap which enables them to absorb water; their succulent leaves give them a place to store it. In addition the long roots and rhizomes which provide a firm anchorage for the plants have special tissue so that they may 'breathe' in the airless mud.

The world of grasses

Whether our tastes are for a waving meadow, or a neatly kept lawn, most of us appreciate the verdant presence of grass without giving it a second thought.

Grass flowers are easily missed because they are so small, and lack the bright petals which attract our attention to other blooms. However, if you take the trouble to look at grasses in the main mid-summer flowering season, you discover a small world of great variety and beauty.

▼ The flowerheads of cocksfoot grow in thick one-sided clumps. Each spikelet has three stamens, which may be yellow or purplish.

Grass pollen as every hay-fever sufferer knows, is wind-borne. Petals would be superfluous in grasses, as with other wind-pollinated flowers such as hazel catkins and fat hen. The flowers of grasses consist simply of stamens—the male parts, and stigmas—the female parts.

Grasses have a huge range of different kinds of flowerheads. Some like timothy, are bunched tightly in a dense brush-like 'spike'. The meadow grasses carry their flowers on a loosely branched spray, and the oat-grasses droop gracefully in a spreading fountain. The stamens generally mature before the stigma and the pollen-bearing anthers are coloured purple or yellow. They protrude beyond the individual spikelets in little hanging clusters to catch the wind. This is what gives summer grass that subtle tinge of colour. The stigmas which, as in all flowering plants, lead to the seed-forming ovary, are white. Their beautiful featheriness gives them the maximum opportunity of catching floating pollen grains.

As with other plants, different species of grass favour different environments. This is often reflected in common names for them, such as wood melick, meadow grass, wall barley, purple moor grass, and alpine cat's tail.

From earliest times to the present day, man has made extensive use of grasses. A lush mixture of rye-grass, cocksfoot, meadow grass and crested dogstail makes a tasty pasture for even the most finicky cows. The bread and flour in every larder are the product of cereal crops: rye, wheat, oats and barley; cultivated varieties of wild grasses. Lawns contain a good proportion of 'bent', a grass which grows in a soft green carpet and can take a lot of heavy treading. The velvety smooth cricket squares and bowling greens also contain this grass or the much sought-after creeping red fescue.

Cocksfoot

Barley

Rye

▲ Cocksfoot is an easily recognisable grass of wasteland and field. It both grows wild and is cultivated for hay and pasture. The dense tufts flower from mid-summer.

▲ Barley is widely grown as a cereal throughout the world. Its commonest wild relative, wall barley, may be found in Europe, North America and Australia.

▲ Rye-grass, a common pasture grass; the stems are very sweet to chew early in the year. Note the way individual spikelets snuggle into the central axis.

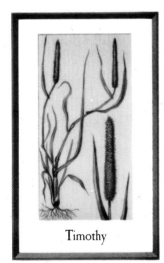

Timothy

Poa

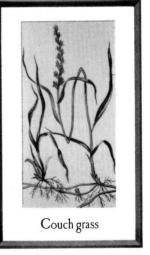

Couch grass

▲ Timothy, a very palatable grass much used for hay and grazing. The common name commemorates Timothy Hansen, who introduced this grass into the United States.

▲ Meadow grass, common in old meadows and by roadsides. It is known as Kentucky Blue-grass in the U.S. and is cultivated for its highly nutritive qualities.

▲ Couch grass, or twitch, is a tough grass. Even a small piece of root-stem can grow up into a separate new plant. Spikelets stick out from the central stem.

Travellers' tales

Botanical annals are full of the tales of intrepid explorers who scoured the world often at great personal risk, in search of new, curious and medically commercial and valuable plants. Many of them are eponymously commemorated in both common and Latin names. The Douglas fir was so-called after the indomitable young Scotsman who brought us many wild flowers and trees from the Pacific coast. Tradescant, gardener to Charles I, gave his name to tradescantia, the popular pot-plant.

As fast as new territories were discovered botanists were there, investigating and taking specimens of the plant resources. One sixteenth century gentleman, a patron and friend of l'Ecluse, the celebrated Dutch botanist, is said to have been so enthusiastic a collector that he set a Turkish prisoner free on condition that he might obtain plants for him from Turkey.

The plant as colonizer

Aided by all this botanical activity, which grew in scope from the sixteenth century onwards with the discovery and exploration of new lands, in the Americas, Australia and the continent of Africa, plants leapt continents and found new centres of distribution in their adopted countries. Many of them, finding the new habitat congenial to growth, spread from the herb gardens and private collections where they were first nurtured. Becoming naturalized, they started to grow wild. By 1600, a number of species brought in from the Near East and Southern Europe—bladder senna, blue sow-thistle and many others—were thriving in a wild state all over Europe.

Lifted from Mount Etna's volcanic dust, Oxford ragwort was sent back as a specimen to the Oxford Botanic Gardens. It quickly colonized the walls of the town.

Railway lines opened up new horizons for plants and people, and this plant readily made its home in the rubble gathered between sleepers, and hitch-hiked by train all over southern England.

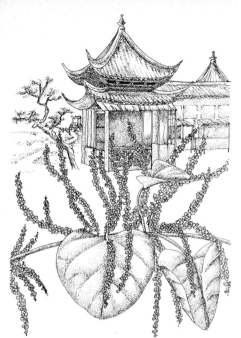

and are carried by birds and animals, often traversing considerable distances to new sites of growth. They also make full use of human transport systems.

An oriental infiltration

The spread of the 'aliens' has in some cases been quite formidable as anyone who has seen the expanding jungles of Japanese knotweed, only introduced into Europe in 1825, will testify. Originally brought over as a garden plant, this bushy alien soon broke bounds, aggressively colonizing roadsides and waste ground. Like many of our most rampant weed-wild-flowers, it reproduces vegetatively as well as by seeds, and is extremely persistent.

▲ Japanese knotweed. This rampant Russian—which it is, despite its nomenclature—was only introduced to Britain in 1825. But it has made its presence felt in gardens and wasteland in no uncertain terms.

Victorian vagrants

The nineteenth century saw more introductions. Buddleia arrived from China. Giant hogweed made its appearance from the Caucasus, Himalayan balsam from India, and the snowberry joined earlier immigrants from North America—orange balsam, Michaelmas daisy and Canadian golden rod.

If the original collectors could see some of their plants now, they would probably be astounded, since plants too are prodigious travellers and colonizers. While the growing plant itself is immobile, its seeds float on the air, travel by water,

▲ The Canadian golden rod was brought to Europe in 1648 as a garden plant. It has become naturalised on wasteland and on railway embankments, providing an autumnal burst of gold.

Wild flowers in lore and literature

Summer is icumen in
Lhude sing cuccu
Groweth seed and bloweth mead
And spryngeth the wood new.

These jaunty lines celebrating the season of plenty comes from one of the oldest known poems in the English language. From classical times onwards, there seems to be scarcely a poet who has not drawn on trees and flowers for inspiration. Many of them, however, simply make use of the natural world for imagery and analogy. The true wild flower writers are those for whom plants have their own individual significance. This includes prose writers as well as poets; look at the early herbalists and gardeners—Gerard, Turner, Parkinson and Miller—as well as the poets, and for more recent writing, turn to Gilbert White and John Clare. Such writers feel no need to 'beautify' wild flowers, nor to romanticise them. Their writing is intensely observed and imaginatively expressed. They capture the essence of their subject.

▼ A beautiful and naturalistic interpretation by Millais of Ophelia's "fantastic garlands" Shakespeare's "crowflower" is probably the ragged robin she clutches in her hand. Other plants represented are yellow-flag and iris, wild and garden rose, and, poignantly, heartsease and forget-me-not.

Lore of the land

Modern science, though it has greatly increased our knowledge of wild flowers, has put a barrier between man and the natural world. People tend to feel that they need a botanical background in order to pursue their interest in plants. Centuries ago, the wild flower landscape was more an integral part of the daily lives of the population. Medicines were derived from wild plants, and people needed to be able to recognise them and to learn their properties, to be able to use the old remedies and 'simples'.

Much of the traditional lore survives. We still use the 'Dock in, nettle out' remedy when we have a brush with stinging nettles. Many people will not bring the lovely sprays of hawthorn into their houses, fearing that it brings bad luck. Country children still eat mallow seeds—'bread and cheese' seeds—and sorrel from the hedgerows. They make daisy chains and play the 'true love' trick, placing the sticky stems of goosegrass on unsuspecting backs. Almost every country has wildflower lore which reveals love, such as counting 'he/she loves me, loves me not' on flower petals. The French version is more complicated—and gives a better chance of coming out on top —'il/elle m'aime, un peu, beaucoup, passionnement, pas du tout'.

The medical knowledge of our ancestors has not been lost. A number of medicaments in contemporary use contain plant substances or a synthetic version of them. Official drug lists contain certain of the old plant drugs: for instance, *digitalis* (present in foxgloves) and *hyoscyamine* and *atropine* (found in deadly nightshade). These derivatives are used in the treatment of heart and stomach ailments. One of the newest and most efficacious, commercially produced treatments prescribed for the relief of asthma, is in fact not so new. It

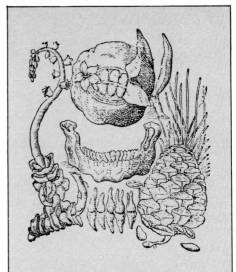

Toothwort and pine cones were both held to be cures for toothache because the hard oval leaf scales and flowers of the toothwort, and the scales of the pine cone, bear a resemblance to teeth. The illustration is taken from the *Phytognomica* of Giambattista Porta, published in 1588. It represented the first attempt at a 'scientific' review of the doctrine of signatures.

This doctrine was based on the idea that while God had permitted the existence of diseases, he had also placed a cure for them near at hand. Accordingly, if a plant resembled a human organ, it could be used to cure an ailment of that part of the body. Such notions gained widespread credence during the sixteenth and seventeenth centuries. The originator of the doctrine was a mystic German doctor, Paracelsus (1493-1541).

uses *inulin*, a drug present in the traditional herb elecampane, which was brought to Britain by the Romans and used from earliest times to treat bronchial complaints.

Flowers in everyday life

In today's closely ordered world, wild plants bring a touch of anarchy and colour to our lives. They follow their own laws not those of human convenience. Whether in the heart of the city, in park or garden flowerbed, or in the depths of country regions, they grow, unplanted and untended. Their wildness invades even the most urbane and civilized precincts.

The influence of wild flowers makes its way inside our homes too. What dwelling is utterly without some form of floral representation, even if only in book decoration, wall-paper, or carpet pattern or picture? True, in decorative art, painters and designers may take liberties with botanical structures. Millais and Burne-Jones took considerable pains to achieve naturalistic and accurate representations of wild plants in their paintings. (These make good subjects for a 'field' survey

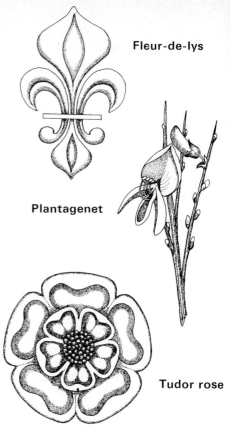

Fleur-de-lys

Plantagenet

Tudor rose

▲ Three flowers which take their place in history as royal emblems. The iris or "flag" is the *fleur-du-lys* of the French; broom the *Planta genista* of the Plantagenet kings, and the Tudor rose, England's emblem, an artificial composite of the roses of York and Lancaster.

◄ The frontispiece of the most famous of English herbals, *The Grete Herbal* of 1526.

on winter days when living plants are not much in evidence.) But their Pre-Raphaelite comrade, William Morris, was not above occasionally ignoring a petal or a perianth section here or there if he found it interfered with the symmetry of his design.

We send flowers as signs of affection, thanks or congratulations, and they are nonetheless potent for being 'Interflora' rather than a hand-gathered posy. Athletes and *Grand Prix* victors are still wreathed in laurels. The custom of laying flowers and wreaths on graves goes back far into antiquity, and it seems unlikely that we shall drop the habit. Even the cinders of the cremated are often buried along with a rosebush.

Regional reminders

A number of relics of wild flower history are still with us in the names of streets and regional names, such as London's St John's Wood and Primrose Hill. There are living relics too; the woodland plants that persist in cleared fields and hedgerows, the crossroad oaks, the yews of churchyard and old garden.

Yew is one of a number of plants said to ward off evil, which may well have been a good reason for planting them near buildings. A herbaceous wildplant with almost as powerful a reputation is the modest Herb bennet, the *Herba Benedicta*, which gives profound protection against all forms of evil. Often found by the wayside, a leaf or sprig of herb bennet was often carried on a journey to afford safety to the traveller.

▶ Three wild flowers—buttercup, hop and hawthorn —from Southwell Cathedral, executed with fine naturalistic skill by anonymous sculptors in the thirteenth century.

A rose by any name

Vernacular names for wild flowers make a fascinating study. Imaginative in their variety, they give an insight into old customs. Equally, anyone who has touched on the subject will feel that the Latin binomial system—alien though it may seem at first —is completely vindicated when it comes to establishing exactly which flower you are talking about. Not only is there often a huge vocabulary of common names— sometimes many for a single plant—in every country where it grows, but the names are not at all consistent. What the

▼ A pictorial interpretation of the Narcissus legend in a German herbal of 1491.

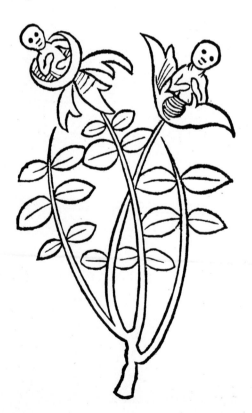

Scots mean by 'bluebell' (*Campanula rotundifolia*) is different from what the English understand it to be—*Endimion non-scriptus* —the familiar spring flower of our woods. The Australian bluebell is different again and America calls at least four species by this common name.

A clue to usage

Names often give an indication of traditional usages of plants. Fullers teasels (also known as "brushes and combs" and "clothes brush") are, even in the twentieth century, still the best means of raising the nap of cloth or the baize on billiard tables. This plant is also known as "Our Lady's basin"—a reference to the cupped form of the bases of the leaves, in which little pools of water gather. Many flowers were dedicated to the Virgin Mary. There is Our Lady's bedstraw, Our Lady's cushion, Our Lady's nightcap; Our Lady's smock, slipper, looking glass, and many more. In fact, almost all her personal requirements have their symbolic representation in the wild flower repertoire.

Medical associations are often recalled by common names. Dandelion, a diuretic, is known in France as 'piss-en-lit' and similarly, in North America as 'pissamire'. A few names are local versions of Latin: the evocative 'gallant soldier' of the waysides sounds as if it should have an interesting history. In a way it has; it is a bastardized form of the Latin name *Galinsoga parviflora*. Ribwort plantain is a plant with a more authentic military association. A game is played with it, all over Europe, matching one flowerhead against another, blow for blow as in conkers, until one head falls off. In England this plant is known as 'conqueror flowers', 'soldiers' and 'men-of-war'. In Sweden it is 'kämpa' and in Danish 'kjampe' meaning warriors.

The language of flowers

▲ The forget-me-not has similar names in most European languages. One legend tells of a knight who called out the phrase as he drowned, clutching the flower.

▼ Lords and ladies, Jack in the pulpit, Cocky baby, are all names for this familiar flower. The phallic shape of the central spandix has made it an emblem of ardour —and something of a naughty joke.

◄ The name Shepherd's purse alludes to the heart-shaped seeds of this common flower, a fit size for a shepherd's wages.

► Jack-go-to-bed-at-noon, or goatsbeard, is a clock plant, which closes its petals early in the day.

▲ Touch-me-not balsam, *Impatiens noli-tangere*, means what it says, even in Latin. It has an explosive— and disconcerting—habit of flinging its seeds out when ripe.

Look - don't pick

Over the centuries, botanists have enthusiastically charted the flora of their own and other countries. Many of the old herbalists and apothecaries used to undertake botanical trips into the surrounding countryside as well as engaging on expeditions to inspect foreign plant life. However, by the end of the nineteenth century, enthusiasm began to get out of hand. There was an outburst of popular interest not only in botany, but in the craze for collecting. Seaweeds and ferns suffered from the marauding attentions of the collectors, and many other wild flowers, especially orchids, suffered depredation.

Nowadays we have learned to be more responsible in our attitude to wild flowers. Britain and a number of other countries have protective legislation against the spoilage of wilderness. This makes it illegal to uproot any wild plant unless one has the permission of the owner of the land it is growing in. There are also 21 species which form a special list. It is absolutely forbidden to uproot, pick or otherwise harm any of these plants.

▶ Four endangered plants of Britain and Europe. Alpine gentian is becoming particularly rare in Britain. The spears of wild gladiolus used to be found in the marshy land of France and Britain, but drainage has made them scarce. The monkey orchid, like others of its species, is suffering from acute depletion. And diapensia a tundra plant, has been affected by a changing climate.

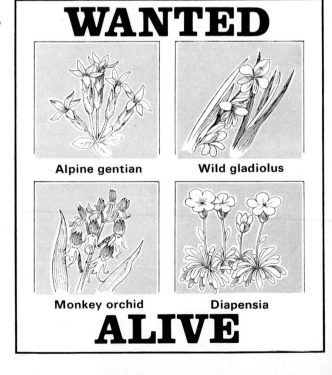

WANTED

Alpine gentian

Wild gladiolus

Monkey orchid

Diapensia

ALIVE

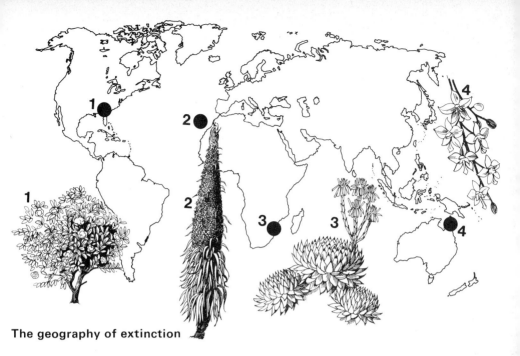

The geography of extinction

Natural history groups, both on a local and national level, devote themselves to surveying, photographing and studying wild flowers in their habitats. Such groups also do a great deal towards conservation. It is no longer collectors who pose the greatest threat to plant life. Moors, fens and marshes are being drained—sometimes unnecessarily over-drained—for commercial purposes and for housing. Widescale use of the private car in country areas is posing problems of erosion where there are no proper car-parks. Satisfactory compromises can often be reached with these and similar problems, but local awareness is essential, if these are to be reached before the damage is done.

Not wisely but too well

It is ironically, sometimes the wildflower enthusiasts themselves who prejudice the survival of rare plants, by failing to recog-

▲ These four plants are threatened natives of very different climes. *Franklinia alatahama*, the "Lost Franklin" (1), was last seen in the southern US in 1803. *Echium pininana* (2) now rare, was once one of the glories of the Canary Islands. *Aloa polyphylla* (3) is one of 500 left in Lestho. The Cooktown Orchid, *Dendrobium bigibbum* (4), the emblem of Queensland, has suffered for its fame.

nise that a plant habitat is a living and organic place. It is no good taking care not to damage a rarity if, while admiring it, the surrounding undergrowth is trampled underfoot, thereby broadcasting the site and depriving the plant of protection. One county recorder has reluctantly refused to allow parties of botanists, even under supervision, to view the rare fen ragwort *(Senecio paludosus)* because of the danger of such damage to a plant which depends on the support of surrounding vegetation.

The quiet orchids

Would you have recognised the flowers on this page as orchids? For most people, the word orchid summons up exotic tropical blooms, showy monsters with petals up to 60cm across. Though European orchids are smaller and subtler than their tropical relatives, their strangely modelled flowers exert a compelling attraction. Orchids—at least some species—are not as rare as is generally believed. You may find several types of marsh orchid growing profusely on wetland. Woodland can boast the bright spring blooms of the early purple, the ghostly helleborine, and ribbony green flowers of the twayblades. Chalk or lime

▲ The common spotted orchid has very long spurs to its flowers, and spotted leaves.

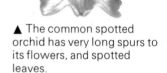

◄ The rose-pink pyramidal orchid bears a dense head of flowers. A photographer's lens also does it justice. ►

▲ The bee-orchid, or "bumble-bee orchis" of open chalky grasslands.

grassland is another good habitat, where fragrant pyramidal and spotted orchids may be discovered—and in some localities bee or butterfly orchids.

Though an extremely large family with a remarkable diversity of form, orchids have one very interesting feature in common. Every species grows in close association with a fungus, to their mutual benefit. This mycorrhizal relationship is vital; orchids will simply not grow without their fungus partner.

Plant dependencies - friend and foe

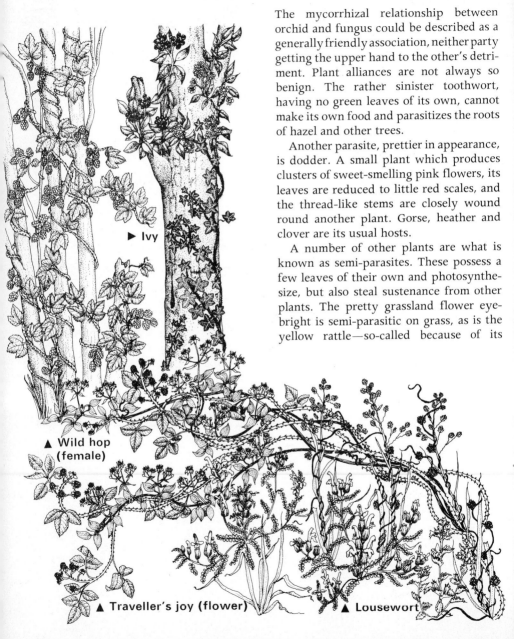

▶ Ivy

▲ Wild hop (female)

▲ Traveller's joy (flower)

▲ Lousewort

The mycorrhizal relationship between orchid and fungus could be described as a generally friendly association, neither party getting the upper hand to the other's detriment. Plant alliances are not always so benign. The rather sinister toothwort, having no green leaves of its own, cannot make its own food and parasitizes the roots of hazel and other trees.

Another parasite, prettier in appearance, is dodder. A small plant which produces clusters of sweet-smelling pink flowers, its leaves are reduced to little red scales, and the thread-like stems are closely wound round another plant. Gorse, heather and clover are its usual hosts.

A number of other plants are what is known as semi-parasites. These possess a few leaves of their own and photosynthesize, but also steal sustenance from other plants. The pretty grassland flower eyebright is semi-parasitic on grass, as is the yellow rattle—so-called because of its pepper-pot seedheads. Mistletoe also falls into this group.

Honeysuckle is not a parasite, though it can be of considerable disadvantage to its host trees and shrubs. Its sinewy stems bind very tightly, cutting deeply into the trunk as it climbs. Young saplings may be killed by this fragrant strangler.

Ivy is a much maligned creeper which causes no harm at all. Being shade-tolerant it can make do with very little light; it does not therefore push itself forward, shading the leaves of its host.

There are a number of other creeping plants which have stems too weak to support themselves unaided. White bryony is most obvious in autumn hedgerows when its tendrils sport glossy red berries. Traveller's joy is also at its best in autumn when it curtains its masses of feathery fruits over trees and shrubs. It does not have tendrils; rather the long stalks of its leaflets are hitched round convenient twigs. Wild hop and bindweed are other well-known climbers of hedgerow and roadside, the first twining itself clockwise—as does honeysuckle—the latter, anti-clockwise.

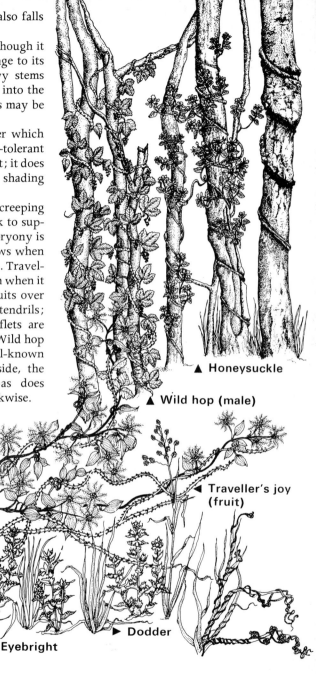

▲ Honeysuckle

▲ Wild hop (male)

◄ Traveller's joy (fruit)

► Dodder

◄ Eyebright

A beginner's guide

One of the nicest things about wild flowers as a pursuit is that you can make it as leisurely or as strenuous as you like. While travelling to work, equipped with no more than a sharp pair of eyes, you can see a lot by just watching the roadsides, walls and waste strips of land. At the other extreme, more rugged enthusiasts can go mountain-climbing or march-tramping in search of wild plants. An intensive study is another option; making a complete flora study of a small area can be a pleasant and absorbing afternoon's task.

Urban botanising

The most important preparation for this activity is to train yourself to recognise likely sites. If you travel a route regularly, watch for the cycle of the opportunist weed-wild flowers; how many generations of flowering and seeding one species can manage, and how many different species succeed each other in the course of a year. Keep a watch too for the 'garden hoppers', flowers which have left the security of gardens to make their own wayward way by wall or roadside.

Most observations may be made without drawing special attention to yourself. However, a hand lens can make life more interesting, and is so small as to be carried without the least inconvenience. Small self-sealing polythene bags are also useful items to carry about with you in case you want to keep a leaf or flowerhead intact, and take it back home to identify. They make excellent containers for seed as well.

▲ The ideal kit. From a Victorian naturalist's guide, Hendschel's *Sketchbook*.

One more fern is popped into the collecting vasculum —one less for posterity.

Country trekking

A trip to the country takes a little more planning, if you want to make the most of it. It is always a good idea to take binoculars with you, not only to get a close look at birds and animals who aren't so obligingly static as wildflowers, but to be able to focus down on those plants glimpsed on the other side of the river, or half way down a steep chasm.

If you were to take field guides to meet any situation you might encounter, you would travel weighted down by a library of references, so only pack your favourite handbook for in-the-field identification. Rely on observation notes, a sketch and, if feasible, an example of leaf or flower. Obviously, if there are only one or two plants of a particular species, you should leave them completely alone. If there is a fair number of healthy specimens, beware that you don't damage a plant when picking a sprig.

How to look at a flower

The great mullein is one you could hardly miss, should you come across it. It grows up to 2 metres in height.

▶ Look closely at the flowers with a hand lens. The green pistil is surmounted by a receptive stigma. Surrounding the pistil are 5 stamens, 3 of which are whitely hairy, and 2 of which are hairless and infertile.

▶ The large leaves, clothed in woolly white down, are probably one of the first things you will notice. The flowers, arranged in a tall dense spike, are yellow and seem almost flat from a distance.

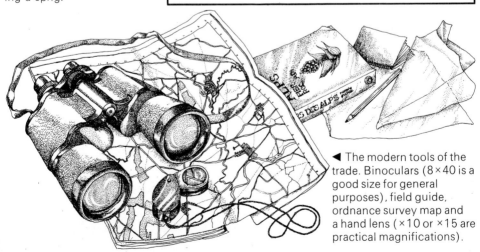

◀ The modern tools of the trade. Binoculars (8×40 is a good size for general purposes), field guide, ordnance survey map and a hand lens (×10 or ×15 are practical magnifications).

Watching for wild flowers

While it soon becomes clear that it is possible to find wild flowers in almost any location, it is quite an art to atune your perceptions so that you quickly become aware of the botanical potential wherever you are. There are different 'ways of looking'. Out on a ramble, you can take your time over examining any plant you come across. On the other hand, when wildflower-spotting from a train or on a motorway, you have to learn to interpret a fleeting patch of colour as it flashes by your window.

Down in the dumps

No aspiring botanist should be too fastidious to investigate a rubbish tip. An excellent selection of exotic aliens often bloom briefly and splendidly on such sites. Birdseed and foreign foodstuffs often contain some marvellous surprises. Look out for cannabis; the beautiful white, pointed flowers of the thornapple; and night-scented evening primrose. You will have as good a chance here as in the open country of seeing kestrels hovering above, and the odd fox in the undergrowth, both doing their own foraging. So don't leave your local tip to Victoriana hounds; lovers of wildflowers unite!

Waterway wildflowers

It is well worth examining a map for stretches of waterway: gravel pits and reservoirs as well as rivers and canals. It is often necessary to apply for a permit to get

into reservoirs, but it is usually a simple procedure of writing to the waterboard concerned which amply repays the effort. Gravel pits too are likely sites for waste-ground flora, and canal banks are often exceptional. These offer a wide range of habitats, from the deeply industrial to the entirely rural, with gloriously overgrown places where canals

have fallen into disuse and the plants have taken over.

If you can actually get on to the water of rivers and canals, boating is a good form of travel for botanists. It affords a close view of waterside plants—and avoids the hazards of slithery banks and wet feet.

Footpaths, fields and forests

Before exploring the more traditional wild flower sites, do a little homework with a map or book on the region. Look for the small rivers, for woods with an irregular outline (these are likely to be

old woods) and for footpaths which cut the contour lines and look as if they pass through a nice variety of habitats. Try to find out the rock composition of the area and if it has any wildflower specialities.

Highways and byways

Railway banks provide sheltered undisturbed places for wildflowers.

It is best to seat yourself in the carriage so as to have a clear view of the sunnier bank. As there is only a second or two at the most to make an observation, you have to learn to sum up what you see. Look for colour, attempt to identify a plant from the general outline of its growth and don't be afraid to make quick decisions about habitats. As

▼ A splendid specimen of "industrial" ragwort. Intruders like this one flourish all over industrial sites in large cities.

▲ A runaway plant straddles the line in a disused siding. Valerians, willowherbs and golden rod are among the intimates of railway life.

you get the hang of this method of observation, railway journeys take on a new aspect; primroses and cowslips at the beginning of the year, through to Michaelmas daisies and Canadian golden rod towards the end.

Motorways, though comparatively new habitats, are beginning to show an encouraging wild flower cover. Within a city the ideal mode of travel is on top of doubledecker buses, from which vantage point you can see over the top of walls into vacant lots, neglected gardens and bridges. There is many a thriving wilderness hidden within corrugated fencing.

Keeping a record

Spring seems to be late this year. Or is it? Surely the celandines, violets and blackthorn were out by this time last year? But no. Turn to your journal; you wait with the same impatience every year for the first flowers.

Keeping a journal is a very good way of building up a record of your natural history observations, whether your taste is for a document of strictly regulated scientific data or a richly evocative personal chronicle.

Other people's records

If you are particularly interested in studying the flora of a specific area, there may be a number of existing records to which you could find access. A local librarian should be able to tell you of any books written about the wild flowers of the region. Many districts also have a herbarium—a collection of dried plants, discovered and collected in the area. Members of the public may on request be allowed to use such collections. Unless you are a confirmed 'loner' you should also contact the local natural history society; records are fascinating, but a group can offer practical assistance on field trips.

Once you have become reasonably confident in your recognition skills, you may see some plant which you think is unusual. (Perhaps it is rare by definition, or growing in a place you would not normally expect to find it.) If this happens, make an accurate note of the location. You might also make a sketch or take a photograph, but certainly take notes of all the main features. If you have a friend who is more expert than you at identification, invite a second opinion. You could also notify your local natural history society, or the county recorder of the BSBI. (The Botanical Society of the British Isles.) Your plant may be on record already—but then again, it may not, and you may have the chance of establishing the first incidence in your county or district. If you are reasonably certain of your identification, you should not be diffident about communicating your observations. Much important work has been achieved by amateur botanists, particularly in the matter of field surveys. The compilers of atlases which show the distribution of wildflowers rely heavily on the sterling work carried out by members of the public who are prepared to send in records from their local areas.

◀ A page from January, 1790, in Gilbert White's journal. Even someone as consciencious as White spilled over the page in his enthusiasm.

Your personal records

There are a number of possible ways of organizing your records. The key is to suit the form to your particular interests.

An ordinary page-a-day diary could be brought into use as a natural history journal and filled up on a volume-by-volume basis. This however, makes cross-reference from one year to another something of a chore.

A large loose-leaf book is one answer, with a page for every day of the year. Each entry is prefaced simply by the year number. This method enables you to compare observations made over a period of years very easily.

Entries could consist of purely scientific data, such as temperature and rainfall, or vegetational changes observed regularly on a particular site. Alternatively, a journal might be a collection of observations of a more

▲ Who would not appreciate a letter like this one, from one naturalist to another in 1792?

▶ Margery Blamey is among the foremost naturallist/illustrators. Her record system is thorough and accurate, including a written description of the plant and its habitat, a specimen and a transparency. But flower pressing is only to be recommended for experts who are aware of rarity potential.

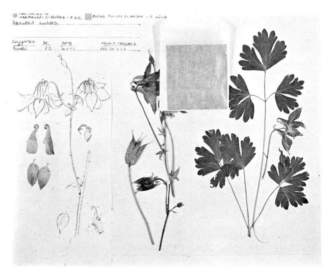

SPECIES NO.	ORDER NO. 1-4	SPECIES NO. 5-9	GENUS & SPECIES 11-24		SUB-SPECIES etc. 10	V.C NO.

VERBASCUM VIRGATUM

GRID REFERENCE 25-32	VICE COUNTY 33-35	LOCALITY 36-55		ALTITUDE 56-57 ft

2 8 6 8 9 5 2 6   Enst Ross   1 0 6   MUNLOCHY BAY   m

HABITAT 58-59	DATE 60-64	RECORDER'S NAME	REC. NO. 65-68

Slope between field and shore   9 8 1 9 7 5   A. Higginbottom

RARITY 69	RARE 1	EXT. 2	CONF. 9	STATUS 70	NAT. 1	INT. 2	ESC. 3	MIG. 4	CAS. 5	SOURCE 71	FLD. 1	MUS. 2	LIT. 3	COMMENTS & COMPILER

STAGE 72	♂ 1	♀ 2	☿ 3	OVA 4	LARV. 5	PUPA 6	SKIN 7	SKEL. 8	ADDITIONAL DATA 90	

First County record - about 12 plants

DETAILS OF SOURCE 73-76	EXPERT 77-79

field   Dr I K Ferguson

IBM 866-22288   NATURE CONSERVANCY

BRC 5-71

general nature; things which have particularly excited and interested you: the first swallow, the daffodil which pushed up a paving stone, how the abundant thistle has brought in huge flocks of goldfinches, details of the flower you observed for a month before you were able to identify it, the cats digging up the fritillary bulbs — again. With such a journal you can watch your progress from the initial tentative gropings, to a more confident and knowledgeable curiousity.

As a quick way of finding particular plant references, it is useful to link your field observations to your journal. All you need is a simple cross reference between field guide and journal. There usually isn't much space for notes in a pocket-sized field guide, but there is enough room for a pencilled date — say 21/4/77 in the margin.

Then on the April 21 page in your journal, you can write a complete entry, with details of where you saw the plant, what struck you about it, observations about habitat etc. This method of recording should gradually become second nature.

Ways of seeing

It almost goes without saying that anyone with an interest in wild flowers is better advised to photograph or sketch a plant than to pick it. Many people forget that to take a bloom is to prevent that flower from producing seeds that year.

Mercifully, the heyday of the plant collector is past. But there are still the thoughtless few who gather armfulls of wild flowers. It was all very well to take a bushel of cowslips to make wine a century ago, but those who fancy going back

▲ A record card for "Twiggy mullein", discovered in August 1975. Information such as this can be fed into a computer for use in distribution maps, etc.

to the old fashioned recipes nowadays, should spare a thought for the fact that cowslips are by no means the common flower they once were.

A good old-fashioned alternative to picking or pressing wild flowers is to paint them. If you are not artistic, follow the practice of painting in a black- and white-printed identification book with the correct colours. This will give a much more lively and pleasing result than the pallid relic of a pressed flower.

Photography

The new wave of botanists, unlike their nineteenth-century counterparts, only take photographs. Flower photography is of course an art, but this should not deter anyone who can afford this now rather expensive hobby. At least one of the most well-known flower photographers started late in life, thinking he'd just like to try his hand at it. Even if your pictures are not up to calendar standard, they will serve as a useful record.

Smile please!

Dissecting a flower

The stem

The leaf

Leaf arrangement

Flower shape

Stems There is a slight degree of curve in every stem. Draw them freehand, even though it's more difficult to get the lines parallel. *NB* Is it a round, square or ridged or winged stem?

Leaves If the leaves are erect sketch the lower ones first, if downward growing, start with the upper leaves. If serrated, draw the serrated outline, before putting in the veins. If lobed, indicate lobes very faintly, then put in ribs and veins and finish drawing in the lobes. When trying to achieve perspective, imagine the leaf skeleton.

Flowers Make sure to place the flower centrally on its stalk. For tubular flowers draw circle, centre and the divisions of the corolla. Draw in the tube to the centre of the flower. For composite flowers, define and outline, subdivide with lines radiating from the centre. Note whether florets are spreading or turned down, toothed or not.

Raising a wild garden

It is no surprise that people who enjoy wild flowers often become discontent with the gaudy garden selection which is the general fashion, and begin to introduce the wild plants back into their gardens. What one is doing though, is making a garden 'wild' only in the sense that the stock is native wildplant seed rather than that of seed packets. It may sound like a contradiction in terms, but a wild garden needs a certain amount of planning and tending if more than a few species are to survive in it.

Selecting the flowers

The first task is to make a list of the flowers you would especially like to have in your garden. Do a little reading on each one, noting things like the flowering and fruiting season, the usual soil requirements and the kind of habitat. Then try to work out the general chances of survival for each plant on your list.

It is worth gambling on a plant's managing to survive in some cases. As we have seen, plants do sometimes flourish against all odds. On the whole, though, try to give your plants an environment which will suit them. There would be little point in planting a species known to dislike lime on chalky soils. However, if you do not have the most desirable situation for a favourite

▶ Some seeds of plants which are fairly easy to find and gather. Don't worry if the seeds cannot be planted immediately; they generally remain viable for some time.

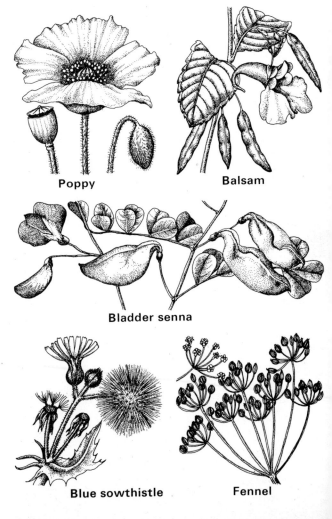

Poppy

Balsam

Bladder senna

Blue sowthistle

Fennel

flower, you might consider ways of creating one. It should not be too difficult to make a pool or an area of shade, but for plants which demand a different soil composition from the one you have, separate containers of some kind are usually the only answer.

There should be enough plants to give your wild flower garden a good start before you have to resort to ingenious artifice. During the summer months, you will have to get used to carrying with you a store of seed containers, in order to be ready for any seed gathering opportunity which presents itself. (Small self-sealing polythene bags are very useful—though not biodegradable. You could also use cellophane bags or envelopes.)

▼ Seed gathering. Stroke the little pods of balsam (a), they curl up like scorpions, releasing their contents. Shake the poppy pots (b) over a bag; pick off the fluffy rosebay seeds (c).

a) Stroke

b) Shake

c) Pick

Gauging ripeness

Beware the commonest mistake, which is to collect seed before it is ripe and ready. Watch the plant carefully; it has its own means of distributing its seed and if you watch for this to begin to come into operation, you will not be tempted into over-eager snatching of immature fruits.

Seed containers such as pods and capsules generally become drier and browner as they mature—until they split, spilling the seed. Pappus-bearing seeds will begin to be tugged at by the wind, and then to start floating away as they ripen. As the fruits of balsams and spurges mature, they dry until they reach the stage where they burst open violently, flinging the seed out. When you gather these, you will have to trigger the fruiting body yourself. The merest touch will set off the reaction when the seed is ripe. Don't squeeze, or it will spring too early and you will find yourself with useless, greeny-white immature seeds instead of plump dark brown ones.

The general rule is: wait for the plant to tell you when it is ready, and learn to recognize the signs. In the case of succulent hedgerow fruits and berries, watch out when the birds begin to take them, then step forward and claim a few for yourself.

Planning and planting

It would look very odd if, having gathered your seeds, you then proceeded to lay them out in neat rows in a herbaceous border. Plants—

especially wild ones—tend to look their best in naturalistic clumps. Before you start sowing seed or planting out seedlings or cuttings, make a survey of your garden, searching out the planting possibilities. By their very nature, wild flowers call for a certain higgledy-piggledyness, but it needs to be a planned disorder rather than a complete wilderness.

Make a note of the sizes of the plants you hope to grow, and whether they are annual,

▼ A view of a romantic country garden, bursting with wild flowers.

biennial or perennial. (You will find this information in any good field guide.) Plan your garden according to shape, colour and size, taking care to give each species its proper requirement in the way of damp, shade and shelter. Field poppies look rather out of place in flower beds, but if you let an area of grass grow and scatter your poppy seed there, you get two advantages. You will have the flowers of the various grasses which make up your lawn, and a lovely background for the poppies.

With most wild plants it is possible to plant straight

Nooks and crannies

▲ The spaces between paving stones make a nice niche for thyme, chamomile, speedwells and sweet alison.

▲ In damp places, by ditches, water butts or taps, grow mint, balsams, and other fen plants.

▲ Walls and steps make a good place for ferns, ivy, ragwort, ivy-leaved toadflax and stonecrops.

Taking a cutting

Elder cuttings may be put in small pots or planted directly in the garden. They "take" readily, and will usually do well in their first year. But they do not flower until they are a good size.

Trim off the larger leaves at the base of the cutting, and make the planting edge diagonal. If planted in a pot use a peaty potting mix.

Be sure not to damage the plant when you take a cutting.

▲ Tend your wild garden well, and you will find it every bit as beautiful and decorative as more orthodox plots.

▲ It can also provide food for butterflies and moths, and a happy-hunting ground for honey-bearing bees,

▲ and you will be doing a service to botanical reserves if you breed pure stocks or "gene banks".

into prepared soil. This often works as well, or even better, than bringing them up to seedling size in small flower pots. The same is true of cuttings, for plants such as rose, elder and hawthorn and others. Divide your seeds into two parts and try both methods. Stick to the one with which you get most success.

If you know of an area where wild flowers grow which is going to be ploughed, or destroyed by developers, contact´ the owner of the land and ask if you may transplant the flowers. (By law you have to ask permission to do this.) By this means you will not only have saved the plants, and

gained some new residents for your garden into the bargain, but these flowers will have the chance of regaining their strength under your care. They may well start colonizing on their own account after a while, spreading to other sites.

Postscript

Don't commit the error of thinking you can leave your wild plants to fend for themselves. As far as is possible cultivate your 'weed-wild-flowers'. Keep nettles (for caterpillars) and thistles (for finches) especially in enclosed places, where they are less able to spread out and engulf other plants.

Conservation opportunities

There are many demands on land; for housing, roads, industry and agriculture. Many of our more critical wild flower habitats would disappear completely if strenuous effort were not made to conserve them. Nature reserves in Britain account for less than 1% of the land, so clearly other kinds of conservation are required as well. But at least there are some places where there is active concern for wild-life and threatened species of plant and animal are cared for.

Keeping nature natural

Some nature reserves are centred around a special group of rare plants, others represent a particular form of threatened habitat, such as fenland or water meadow. Many reserves have nature trails and open days for the benefit of the general public. If your interest extends to putting in some practical effort in the running of nature reserves, your help will probably be received gratefully. Get in touch with your local natural history group, or one of the conservation bodies; they should be able to advise you about the requirements in your area.

A certain amount of experimental work goes on at nature reserves. One Naturalists' Trust in Cambridgeshire carried out long-term observations on different kinds of management of an area rich in marsh orchids. After ten years, it was clear that the strips which had been lightly grazed by cows and horses showed the best results, even out-doing a strip where the surrounding sedges were kept to the right level by selective cutting by hand.

Although there are many tales of woe—plants protected by law being uprooted, habitats being ravaged —there are moves on the positive side too. Public awareness of the need for conservation seems to be increasing. Government

Habitats you may want to conserve

Rocks

Quarry

Woodland

Moorland

Permanent pasture

Stone wall

Boulder slope

Island

Stream

Reservoir

Hedgerow

Bog

▲ A guide to habitats found on any hill farm which are worth conserving. Pamphlets with information on farm nature reserve schemes are published by several provincial naturalists' trusts. Owners are encouraged to submit their land to a survey by wildlife experts.

◄ Primrose planting on a roadside bank in Devon. The plants come from a flower-covered hillside which was due to be ploughed.

grants are available for the setting up of reserves and for tree-planting projects.

A number of rather special reserves have also been put on record; these are roadside verges, listed as 'sites of outstanding botanical interest'. Amateur botanists should always keep a lookout for roadside sites where interesting vegetation may be at risk. Such places should be reported to the local Naturalists' Trust.

Wild flower enthusiasts can contribute to the protection and conservation of plants in a number of ways, and insignificant as it may

seem on the individual scale, a wild garden helps a bit. There are not so many nature reserves, but there are 600,000 gardens in Britain alone. These could contribute even more than they already do, to maintain a good balance of wildlife. Try thinking of your garden as a miniature nature reserve.

Replanting
All over the industrial world, there are unsightly sores left by abandoned workings, buildings and waste heaps, and disused transport sys-

tems like canals and railways. Left to themselves, canals and railways would begin to show an interesting array of wildflowers after only a few years. With the demand for land however, these places are usually quickly seized and built upon, and lose their wildlife potential. However, a number of groups of concerned naturalists have put up a fight for old railway lines and in many cases won the local community a nature trail or a 'linear park'.

▼ A group from an adult education class make a close study of the greater plantain, growing in a gutter.

Some industrial sites are barren by nature. It would take a very long time for a quarry-working or a slag heap to recolonize naturally. Work is being done in such industrial wastelands by groups of botanists and by conservation - conscious schools. This entails a good deal of manual labour, clearing the ground of rubbish and waste ground plants, and replanting with species suitable for the area. The seedlings and saplings then need to be tended until they are properly established. It is a long job, but some of the results have been extremely satisfying.

Local groups and school-children have also contributed a great deal of imaginative effort and hard work to repairing some of

the damage done by heavy bulldozers in road-widening schemes. This involves taking up the existing wild flower resources before the road-making machinery arrives, and replanting elsewhere. When the new road is completed, a new round of collecting and planting wild flower seed and plants (from special reserves or threatened areas), begins.

One of the most unusual innovations in wild-flower conservation is the cemetery nature trail. Far from being morbid places, some of the older cemeteries— not spoiled by a fetish for rigidly neat flowerbeds and lawns—are pleasantly overgrown. In these quiet surroundings and extremely fertile soil, the plants may thrive undisturbed.

Individual initiative

There is a variety of small but important projects which are being tackled by groups of individual enthusiasts. These include the cleaning and recolonization of ponds, conservation and plant surveying in churchyards and on golf-courses. Unlikely though it may seem at first, these places represent important wild flower ressources. In particularly built-up areas, they may be the only stretches of land, other than waste land, where wild-flowers can get a footing.

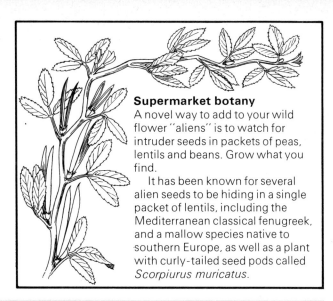

Supermarket botany

A novel way to add to your wild flower "aliens" is to watch for intruder seeds in packets of peas, lentils and beans. Grow what you find.

It has been known for several alien seeds to be hiding in a single packet of lentils, including the Mediterranean classical fenugreek, and a mallow species native to southern Europe, as well as a plant with curly-tailed seed pods called *Scorpiurus muricatus*.

ALIEN HUNTING

It is easy to catch the enthusiasm for "alien" hunting. One often comes across these wild flower visitors in unexpected sites, but there are certain kinds of places which tend to be particularly fruitful. Look out for spots such as these listed below which may house special types of alien flora.

Wool factory dumps

Wool shoddy carries a large number of plant aliens. At one dump in Yorkshire a number of Australian plants were found thriving, including *Abutilon theophrasti* and *Erodium crinitum*.

Airstrips

Aliens are sometimes carried in on aeroplane wheels or with freight. At a small airfield in southern England, *Erigeron strigosus*, a Michaelmas daisy-like plant from N. America, seems to have established a thriving colony.

Sportsfields and verges

Imported grass-seed sometimes contains some interesting aliens, both grasses and other flowering plants. Fifty plants of *Abutilon theophrasti* have been spotted on a single strip of verge, and common flax (*Linum usitatissum*) is often found in these sites.

Docksides

Imported goods often carry alien seeds. Some plants which have been seen at docksides are: Amaranthus, Hibiscus, green nightshade and broomrape.

Tips of factory waste

There can be interesting outcrops of aliens which derive almost entirely from a particular import. For instance in soya beans brought in from the US were found a species of amaranth from Argentina; morning glory, a related species, *Ipomoea hederacea*, and specimens of American cocklebur—a troublesome weed of soya bean crops.

Golf courses

These provide nice sheltered habitats for plants and aliens (such as *Spiraea*, well-known to gardeners) which quite often becomes naturalized there.

Meadow browsing

While every lover of wild flowers would oppose wholesale plundering of the countryside's resources on a large scale, no-one objects to black-berrying, or gathering a few sloes for sloe gin, or some herbs and greens to add to a salad. It is not a matter of serious hunger but of a relish for the wild foods and the pleasure of seeking them out.

There is much pleasure to be gained in simply nibbling your way through the countryside. There are all sorts of edible treats in store on a country walk. Try the thin spicy leaves of hedge garlic, the tender munchiness of young cow-parsley, the tangy 'green-apple' taste of sorrel. If you're by the sea, savour the salty succulence of sea-purslane and aniseed-flavoured alexanders. All

these 'wild greens' make excellent salad ingredients.

Look out for ways also in which you can add wild-plant delicacies in small quantities to everyday cooking. There is a large range of wild plants you can eat and they can add a delicious seasonal variety to your diet. Gather and use wild produce in the same way as you might add herbs or spice, or as an extra vegetable.

Of course it is extremely important to know exactly what it is you are picking. Don't take short cuts with identification if you are thinking of eating a plant. You have to be sure you are gathering cow-parsley and not hemlock, or the equally poisonous hemlock water dropwort.

This said however, once you are certain about the identity of your plant, be as

Elder flowers/berries

▼ Elder is a marvellous bush. Put a flowerhead in with a sweet jam as you cook it. This gives a delicious nutty flavour to apricot or plum preserves. Add whole elderberries to jam and pies.

Elderflowers and jam

Meat flavouring

▼ Add dandelion leaves or chopped horse-radish to meat dishes while they are roasting. Dandelions, chopped with thyme and other herbs, makes a tangy stuffing for beef. As an accompaniment, try fat hen, chickweed or marsh samphire, lightly sautéed in a little butter.

Meat flavouring

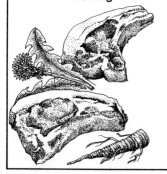

imaginative and experimental as you like. Don't be bound by the restrictions of recipes; use their ideas by all means, but then go on to discover your own taste blends and food combinations.

Think of all the ways the ubiquitous dandelion may be used. It grows plentifully, throughout the year; it is richer in minerals than most shop-sold vegetables, and could be a marvellous resource for the kitchen if you can find ways you enjoy eating it.

The taste of dandelion is bold and sharp. The leaves are an obvious asset in salad, but try putting them in with mincemeat, or adding them to the last stages of a stew. Alternatively match one strong taste with another. A delicious snack is the dandelion roll, made of a largish leaf wrapped up with grilled bacon, or Stilton cheese.

Wrapping food

Fish and butter

▲ Try cooking fresh fish on a bed of fennel. Mackerel and herring taste wonderful grilled or baked in this way.

An old use of butterbur was as a wrap for butter. The leaf veins make an interesting pattern on the soft butter. Nowadays, its large leaves also make an excellent cover to cheeses and condiments on a picnic.

Salad specials

▼ A salad surprise. Don't disregard basic lettuce, tomato and spring onions, but don't be afraid to add cow parsley and dandelion or fennel, mint and the young leaves of hawthorn, lime or beech. All of these, tossed in a light dressing of salt, pepper, oil, vinegar and mustard, make a refreshing flavour change.

Early salad

How to use an ID book

The thrill of discovering a new flower for the first time can have a frustrating counterpoint for the novice, baffled in the search to identify the find. These few pages offer practical hints in the hope of reducing the confusion. There are a number of simplified and selective flowerbooks on the market but on the whole these are probably best avoided. It is better to devote a little time to learning how to use a good field guide sensibly and systematically. It will save a lot of irritation in the long run and there is a great deal of satisfaction in making a careful examination of a plant and being able to work out where in the field guide you will discover its identity.

The golden rule

The first rule is *always to take the book to the flower, not the flower to the book.* Apart from the fact that picking flowers is not advisable (the plant may be harmed and the flower will quickly go rank and die anyway), if you work on the spot, you will be able to check all the identification points against the plant as a whole. If you don't have your field-guide handy, the next best thing is to try to memorize or sketch the most distinctive characteristics of the plant: general aspect, leaf shape, flower shape and colour, hairiness, prickliness and so on.

▲ Excerpts from two good field guides. Above, the chickweed illustrations from the book by the Reverend Keble-Martin . . .

▶ and part of the "Chickweeds and Allies" key from the Fitter, Fitter and Blamey field guide, published by Collins.

Another point to bear in mind is that, seductive though the pictures might be, you should use them only as a rough guide. Always read the relevant piece of text carefully before you decide on your identification. The text will list all the main identification features. Some of these you may have missed in the illustration, although it may superficially resemble the plant you have found.

Size is often particularly difficult to assess. You could find a picture which fits exactly, only to discover in the text that the plant in question is five times larger than the one you are seeking to identify. The text should also contain useful information about typical habitats and flowering seasons.

Choosing your books
There are a large number of excellent field-guides available.

They vary considerably in approach and complexity. The ultimate work of botanical reference is Clapham, Tutin and Warburg's *Flora of the British Isles,* but this is really too technical for a beginner, as well as being far too big to carry around. Most people find the handbook field-guides are perfectly satisfactory for most purposes. (There are descriptions of some of these on p95.) Which one suits you best is really a matter of experience and personal taste: some people like photographic representations, others get on better with illustrations. A personal choice is the Fitter/Blamey *Wildflowers of Britain* paperback for use in the field, to be cross-checked against other references on return home.

Finally, a word about local floras. These vary in standard, but are usually well worth

consulting if you are interested in looking in detail at the plants of a particular area.

▼ A page showing the distribution of mistletoe over Europe from the *Atlas Florae Europeae,* a major work published in 1976. Black dots represent areas where the plant is native; white dots, introduced outcrops; and crosses, where it is extinct or thought to be so.

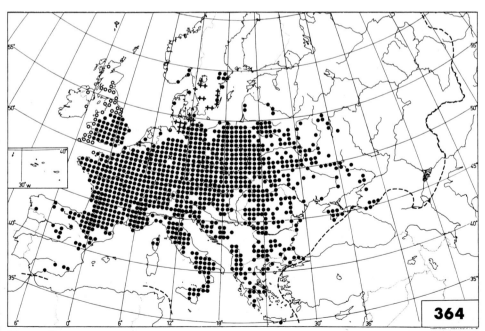

Viscum album

First steps

Unless you're going to be a sitting-room botanist you will one day have to put your powers of observation to the test. So field-guide in hand, you're face to face with an interesting-looking plant. But where do you start? Your field guide has 1000 species or more listed. How do you go about isolating the one you want to identify?

You could, of course, make your way painstakingly through the field guide, looking for a plant which resembles your specimen. This method is not only tedious, but full of pit-falls. There are always non-visual aspects you can overlook.

Long shot

Let's look at the plant in long shot in two senses. First take a step back and simply look at the plant and ponder it. Try to get a sense of its character. Is it short or tall, stemmy or leafy, single or multi-flowered? Then keeping all these things in the back of your mind make a 'long-shot' guess at what family it belongs to.

This is not such a hit-and-miss method as it may sound. Plants are grouped into families because they share certain characteristics, and these are often most obvious when you look at the whole plant. This essential character of a plant is known as 'jizz'. 'Jizz' is a kind of internalized science, and we do it all the time with plants and birds we know well. We don't, for instance, rush to a reference book when we see a sparrow or a dandelion. We know what they are because we have seen them many times before, we have imprinted on our minds a picture of what these species are. It is only a step to go from flowers you know, to those which are unfamiliar. Is it dandelion-like (*Compositae*), hogweed-like (*Umbelliferae*), buttercup-like (*Ranunculaceae*) and so on.

This method is not infallible. You may not have picked out the definitive group of characteristics from a plant, and there are always the exceptions: the untypical members of any family. But your mistakes will be interesting ones and you will learn from making them. And all things considered, it is much more pleasing to 'jizz' out the identity of a plant than it is to spell out its separate tiny features of identification and add them up—though close-work is necessary when you come to discriminate between separate species of the same family—and this has its own special satisfactions too.

LATIN CLUES

The second part of many Latin names is descriptive and often gives a useful hint about the character of the plant. Below are a few common epithets:

Relating to habitat:
aquaticus—of water
arvensis—of fields
maritimus—of the sea
muralis—of walls
nemorosa—of woodland
montanus—of mountains
palustris—of marshes
veris—spring flowering
vulgare—common

Relating to character:
albus—white
asper—rough
esculentus—edible
foetidus—stinking
glomeratus—crowded
glutinosus—sticky
humilis—low growing
hirsutus—hairy
impudicus—lewd
inflatus—swollen
inutilis—useless
irritans—causing discomfort
imbecillis—feeble
maximus—largest
nutans—nodding
officinalis—of medicinal use
oppositifolius—opposite leaved
ornatis—showy
repens—creeping
sempervirens—evergreen
trivialis—ordinary

Bulbous buttercup (Ranunculus bulbosous)

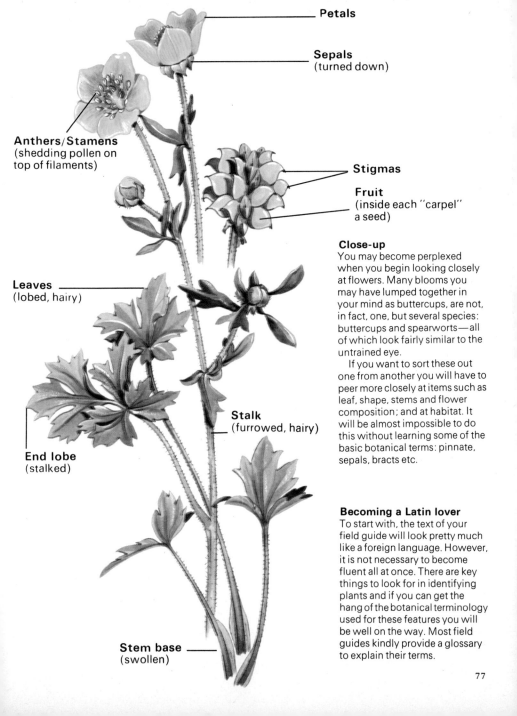

Petals

Sepals
(turned down)

Anthers/Stamens
(shedding pollen on
top of filaments)

Stigmas

Fruit
(inside each "carpel"
a seed)

Leaves
(lobed, hairy)

Stalk
(furrowed, hairy)

End lobe
(stalked)

Stem base
(swollen)

Close-up

You may become perplexed
when you begin looking closely
at flowers. Many blooms you
may have lumped together in
your mind as buttercups, are not,
in fact, one, but several species:
buttercups and spearworts—all
of which look fairly similar to the
untrained eye.

If you want to sort these out
one from another you will have to
peer more closely at items such as
leaf, shape, stems and flower
composition; and at habitat. It
will be almost impossible to do
this without learning some of the
basic botanical terms: pinnate,
sepals, bracts etc.

Becoming a Latin lover

To start with, the text of your
field guide will look pretty much
like a foreign language. However,
it is not necessary to become
fluent all at once. There are key
things to look for in identifying
plants and if you can get the
hang of the botanical terminology
used for these features you will
be well on the way. Most field
guides kindly provide a glossary
to explain their terms.

Five first families

The next few pages illustrate some of the most common members of a few plant families. The five families have been selected because they have obviously different characteristics. A few species within each family are also shown to indicate family resemblance and to point up the kinds of features one looks for when making a species identification. (The list is by no means exhaustive, nor are the descriptions as complete as those of a field-guide.)

THE UMBELLIFERS

The *Umbelliferae* are a large family, most of them characterized by the 'umbel' or umbrella shape of their flowerheads. The flowers are usually white, sometimes—as in the case of wild carrot—with a pink tinge. A few species such as alexanders, fennel and lovage have yellow-green flowers.

Features to look for
Stems: of umbellifers are often furrowed.

Leaves: are usually arranged in an alternating arrangement up the stem. Where the leaf stem joins the main stem there may be a sheath (see hogweed picture on opposite page). Most umbellifers have divided leaves, that is the edges are deeply cut, rather than presenting a 'simple' line along the edge. (Marsh pennywort with its wavy, round, simple leaf is an exception to this rule.)

Flowers: the tiny flowers are clustered together in groups to form the umbel. Each is five-petalled, usually with a notch in each petal. Petals may be of unequal sizes. In each flower there are five stamens.

Fruits: the fruits form beneath the flowers. When the flowers wither there is an umbel of fruits. They vary considerably from species to species and can be important in making a precise identification.

Possible confusions
Elder (*Sambucus nigra*): confusion may occur if flowerheads alone are compared. Elder flowers, too, come in creamy-yellow heads. However, elder is a woody shrub, its exuberant, spreading manner of growth distinctly different from the smaller umbellifer clumps.
    Looking closely it may be observed that the leaves of elder grow opposite each other up the stems (not alternately) and that each individual flower has its petals joined into a tube at the base.

Yarrow (*Achillea millefolium*): flowers also grow in umbel-like heads, but close examination will show that there are five outer 'disc' florets and several yellow, inner 'ray' florets—putting it in the family compositae. The feathery dark green leaves are aromatic when bruised.

▲ Wild Carrot (*Daucus carota*) flower umbels concave, fruit umbels more so, the outer held much higher than the inner ones so there is a hollow in the centre, like a bird's nest. There may be a single pink flower in the centre of the white ones. Lower bracts are much forked.
—grassy places, especially near the sea.

▲ Shepherds needle (*Scandix pecten-veneris*). Fruits long and thin in a comb-like arrangement. Upper bracts (just beneath flowers) forked, no lower bracts.
—on waste ground, fields.

▲ Hemlock (*Conium maculatum*). Tall plant, hairless, smells unpleasantly musky. Stems smooth, spotted with purple. Upper bracts on the outside of the umbel only.
—damp grassy places.

The common hogweed

▼ Pignut (*Conopodium majus*).
Usually quite short, slender in
habit. Upper leaves delicately

threadlike.
—open woods, shady grassland,
rare on lime.

▲ Alexanders (*Smyrnium
olustatrum*). Tall, generous
plants with pungently aniseed
smell. Leaves trefoil (in three
leaflets), deep green and glossy.
Flower heads yellow-green,
fruits black.
—hedgebanks and waste
ground near the sea.

▼ Angelica (*Angelica
sylvestris*). Generally tall, the
flower umbel in an almost
globular arrangement. Stems

often purple coloured. Note
large inflated sheaths on leaf
stalks.
—damp grassy places and
woods, cliffs.

GERANIUM FAMILY

The *Geraniaceae* include cranesbills and storksbills, so-called because their fruits have a long 'beak'. They are generally hairy or even downy. The flowers have five equal-sized petals which sometimes have notches in them. Leaves have stipules at the base of leaf stalks.

Immediately below the petals are five sepals, sometimes ending in a bristly tip, as in shining cranesbill (*Geranium lucidum*). Both cranesbills and storksbills have ten stamens, but in storksbills only five have pollen-bearing anthers.

Features to look for
Leaves: lobed or 'cut' to a greater or lesser extent in different species.
Fruits: beaked, sitting upright within the cup of the sepals.

Petals: whether these are notched or not is important in telling species apart.

▼ Meadow cranesbill (*Geranium pratense*). Tallish plant of grassy places. Flowers a distinctive blue, petals with a central peak rather than a notch. Fruit smooth, beak about 2.5cm. As with other cranesbills, the lobes of the fruit flick upwards when ripe, literally throwing out the seeds.

THE DAISY FAMILY

The *Compositae* are the largest family of flowering plants. The tightly packed flowerhead is enclosed by sepal-like bracts. The florets are of two kinds, disc florets which have five small teeth at the top of the petal-tube, and ray florets which have a long flat strap on one side. The tiny fruits usually have a feather 'pappus' which floats in the air.

Features to look for
Flowers: Are flowers composed of ray florets, disc florets or a mixture of both?

Leaves: Do leaves clasp the stem, are they opposite, or in a rosette? Are they prickly?

Stems: Are stems 'winged' with prickles?

Geraniums

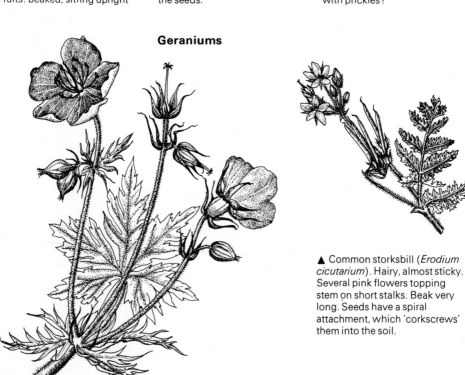

▲ Common storksbill (*Erodium cicutarium*). Hairy, almost sticky. Several pink flowers topping stem on short stalks. Beak very long. Seeds have a spiral attachment, which 'corkscrews' them into the soil.

80

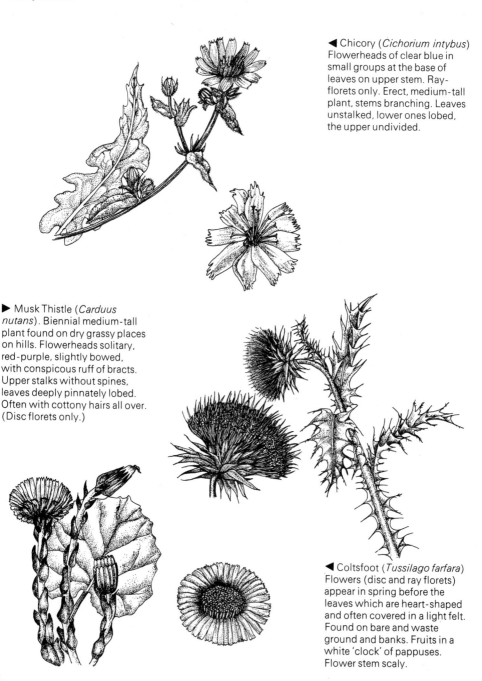

◀ Chicory (*Cichorium intybus*)
Flowerheads of clear blue in
small groups at the base of
leaves on upper stem. Ray-
florets only. Erect, medium-tall
plant, stems branching. Leaves
unstalked, lower ones lobed,
the upper undivided.

▶ Musk Thistle (*Carduus
nutans*). Biennial medium-tall
plant found on dry grassy places
on hills. Flowerheads solitary,
red-purple, slightly bowed,
with conspicous ruff of bracts.
Upper stalks without spines,
leaves deeply pinnately lobed.
Often with cottony hairs all over.
(Disc florets only.)

◀ Coltsfoot (*Tussilago farfara*)
Flowers (disc and ray florets)
appear in spring before the
leaves which are heart-shaped
and often covered in a light felt.
Found on bare and waste
ground and banks. Fruits in a
white 'clock' of pappuses.
Flower stem scaly.

81

Two common labiates

The *Labiatae*—from the latin, meaning lip—include the mints and nettles. Plants in this family have square stems, from which the flowers grow usually in whorls at the bases of the leaves. The flowers themselves are commonly two-lipped, as in nettles, but the mint-type flowers show a more open, lobed configuration. The sepals are joined in tubes. Many labiates are aromatic: mint, wild basil, majoram, thyme, pleasantly so; others like horehound and woundwort, may take some getting used to.

Features to look for

Leaves: All labiates have simple leaves, growing opposite each other up the stem. They may be narrow, heartshaped, toothed— with or without stalks.

Flowers: A range of colours. Commonly one or two-lipped, but can show open, lobed shape.

Stems: always square.

▲ Marjoram (*Origanum vulgare*) pleasantly aromatic, small, softly downy herb. Flowers purple, in clusters at the top of branched stems. Leaves oval, sometimes slightly toothed. Chalky grassland.

◀ White dead-nettle (*Lamium album*). Short, hairy creeping perennial. Not branched. Flowers white, in whorls at base of leaves. Leaves heart-shaped, toothed, stalked. Faintly aromatic. Found on waysides, waste ground.

THE PEA FAMILY

The best recognition feature of the pea family *Leguminosae* is the distinctive pea-type flower. The members of this family vary a great deal in size—from large trees such as false acacia, to low-growing undershrubs such as clover.

Features to look for

Flower: With minor variations, it consists of a broad 'standard' on the top, two narrower 'wing' petals, and a lower 'keel', two joined petals in which lie the stamens and styles. May be in spikes, clusters or solitary.

Stems: May be spiny—e.g. gorse, restharrow; or ridged or winged.

Leaves: Many different kinds: trefoil, as in clovers; pinnate (vetches and bladder senna), or spiny. Are there tendrils?

Fruits: Pods—may be inflated, hanging, warty, or twisted into balls or spirals.

Three familiar peaflowers

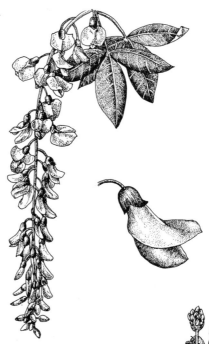

▲ Laburnum (*Laburnum anagyroides*). This member of the pea-family is a tree, growing to 7 metres. Leaves are delicate, trefoil. Flowers yellow, in drooping, leafless spike.

▶ Black medick (*Medicago lupulina*). Short plant, has trefoil leaves. Flowers in round head, pods in coils.

◀ Broom (*Cytisus scoparius*). A deciduous shrub—as opposed to gorse and other pea evergreens. Yellow flowers are carried in leafy spikes. Leaves trefoil. Stems ridged. Fruit, a pod.

Flowers and insects

Pollination is an essential stage in flower reproduction. It occurs when pollen (the male reproductive cells) from the anthers falls on to the stigma (the female part of the flower). If the pollen is compatible—i.e. acceptable to the flower—the pollen grain will grow a tube in reaction to substances produced by the stigma. This tube will penetrate the female ovale. Fertilization takes place when male and female cells fuse. Then the seed begins to form.

Generally speaking, it is best for a plant to be cross-pollinated, and insects are most important in bringing this about, transporting the pollen of one flower to the stigma of another—of the same species but on a different plant. Some flowers have ways of ensuring that self-pollination takes place if cross-pollination has not occurred; pollen falls on to the stigma of its own flower. Certain flowers are 'self-incompatible', and cannot be fertilized by their own pollen. Others, like the bee orchid, are regularly self-pollinated.

As you might imagine, from the huge diversity of flower shapes and forms and the vast range of insect species, the story of plants and their insect visitors is rich and complex. A small selection is presented on these pages.

Lords and Ladies

This pitcher-shaped plant has a large hooded bract which surrounds a central 'spadix'. This exudes a faecal smell attracting small insects such as owl midges. These insects, lured into the slippery hood, slide down the walls into the chamber below. They fall straight down to the bottom where there are a number of female flowers. If one of the insects has come from another lords and ladies plant and is carrying pollen, fertilization will take place as the insects scramble over the flowers. After pollination, changes take place within the plant and the insects trapped in the bottom find themselves able to escape. At the same time however, the anthers of the male flowers mature and as the insects make their escape they are dusted with pollen.

Lords and ladies and owl midges

Heartsease and Queen of Spain Fritillary

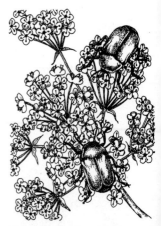

Hedge parsley and leaf beetles

Heartsease

Flowers of the violet family are pollinated only by butterflies and bees with the long probosces necessary to reach the nectar contained in the spur formed by the lower petals. The ovary lies in the centre of the flower, with the stamens clustered about it. Because of certain structural adaptations self-pollination is avoided. The viola also produces small flowers which do not open. These fertilize themselves.

Hedge parsley

Though the individual flowers of umbellifers are tiny, when grouped together in quantity, the flowerheads are very conspicuous to insects. There is a plentiful supply of easily-obtainable nectar, which attracts a variety of insects, including flies, wasps, bees, butterflies, beetles and ants.

Honeysuckle

This fragrant vine is a plant for hovering insects with long probosces. In the late afternoon its nectar tube fills up. At this stage bees can reach the nectar, but by evening when the level has fallen, only very long-tongued creatures like limehawk moths can sip at it, attracted to the flower by its strong night scent. The stamens ripen before the stigma, so self-pollination is avoided.

Yellow flag

This member of the iris family has three large base petals which act as insect landing stages. These are surmounted by three large stigma lobes which each form a channel down which insects crawl to feed, passing the receptive stigma lip and anther as they go.

Flowering rush

Hornets in particular like the blooms of the flowering rush but other insects such as bees, flies and bumblebees also visit throughout the flowering period. The stamens ripen in two stages, first the outer six, then the inner three. It is a flower which self-pollinates if cross-pollination does not occur.

Flowering rush and wasp

Yellow flag and bumble bee

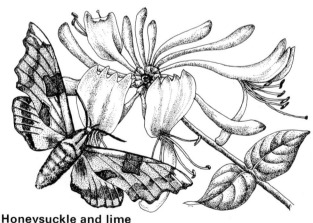

Honeysuckle and lime hawk moth

Flowers and animals

Even the most ardent and single-minded botanist can't ignore the fact that wildflowers are part of a larger ecological pattern. There is obviously considerable inter-relationship between plants and the animals for whom they provide food and shelter. Nor is it a one way benefit: many wild flowers increase their area of distribution by means of birds and insects and mammals. Obvious examples are the hooked burrs of goosegrass and burdock which catch in animal fur, and may travel considerable distances before they are at last scratched out. Other seeds are transported inside birds and animals, who eat and excrete them. Far from harming the seeds' viability, this passage has proved in a number of plants—including fat hen and ribwort plantain—to increase the chances of germination.

There are some interesting anomalies within plant-animal relationships. For instance, birds such as thrushes can eat yew with impunity, while to human beings it is poisonous. In this case the explanation is that the yew seed in the centre of the berry (or aril) of the yew, passes through the bird's digestive system too quickly to be digested, whereas the human metabolism proceeds at a slower rate. There is however no reason known as yet to explain how rabbits appear to be able to feed off deadly nightshade bushes without harm. All parts of this plant are deadly poisonous to people—as indeed is a rabbit who has recently consumed nightshade.

There is a very great deal yet to be observed and studied about the relationships between even our most common animals and plants.

The following sections indicate briefly some of the food plants of a few birds, insects and mammals. In most cases the animals feed from a variety of plants, but in a few cases, there is a strong species dependency as with small tortoise-shell caterpillars and nettles, and brent geese and zostera grass.

Spear thistle and goldfinch

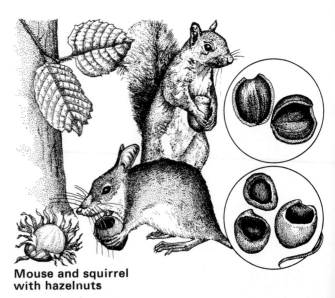

Mouse and squirrel with hazelnuts

Birds

Hawthorn berries, guelder rose berries, and hips—birds of the hedgerow, finches, sparrows, redwings.
acorns—jays
birch seeds—redpolls
thistles and michaelmas daisies —finches (especially gold-finches)
pine and fir cones—crossbills
pondweeds—teal mallard and other ducks
grasses in general—duck, coot and geese.
apples—starlings
fat hen, goose-foot—as you'd expect from the names, used to feed chickens and geese, but a variety of other birds also enjoy the seeds.

Butterflies

These need very little food as adults, but their caterpillars require a good deal of green ruffage. The following plants are those which form the main diet of some of the commoner caterpillars:
nettle—comma, peacock, red admiral and many more
grasses—wall, meadow brown, speckled wood butterflies
sorrel and knotgrass—small copper
oak—green oak moth
bedstraw—hummingbird hawkmoth
violet—dark green and silver washed fritillaries.
Adult butterflies and moths may be seen sipping nectar from a number of plants, in particular buddleia.

Mammals

Hazel nuts and acorns—red and grey squirrels, bank vole, long-tailed field mouse. It is possible to tell the animal which feasted off a hazelnut. Squirrels crack shells apart—often in halves—while the field mouse nibbles uneven holes.
The rarer dormouse leaves neat round holes.
heather moss, grass—red deer, wallabies
Berries—mice, bank vole, badger.
grass and herbs—rabbits, hares.

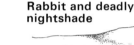

Rabbit and deadly nightshade

Hawfinch and guelder rose fruit

Red deer in heather

Soils and their plants

CHALKY SOILS

Rocky	Grass	Fenland
Open ground and fields		
Alpine penny-cress	Autumn gentian	Cabbage thistle
Buckler mustard	Bee orchid	Common comfrey
Dark red helleborine	Clustered bellflower	Early marsh orchid
Hairy rock-cress	Common spotted orchid	Fen orchid
Pellitory-of-the-wall	Dwarf thistle	Greater spearwort
Rock stone crop	Fairy flax	Marsh bedstraw
Spiked speedwell	Fragrant orchid	Marsh cinquefoil
Sticky catchfly	Greater hawkbit	Marsh helleborine
Stone bramble	Hairy violet	Marsh pea
Wallflower	Horseshoe vetch	Marsh valerian
Whitlow grass	Pyramidal orchid	Milk parsley
	Rock rose	Water chickweed
	Salad burnet	Yellow loosestrife
	Wild candytuft	
Scrub and low bush		
Blackthorn	Dogwood	Alder buckthorn
Hazel	Hawthorn	Blackcurrant
Traveller's joy	Spindle tree	Buckthorn
	Sweet briar	Grey willow
	Wayfaring tree	Goat willow
	Wild privet	Guelder rose
Woodland		
Whitebeam	Ash	Alder
Wych elm	Beech	Birch
Yew	Crabapple	Hawthorn
	Field maple	
	Lime	
	Wild cherry	
Field layer		
Broad-leaved willowherb	Alpine ragwort	Comfrey
Enchanter's nightshade	Bird's nest orchid	Dewberry
Herb bennet	Dog's mercury	Hedge bindweed
Herb robert	Fly orchid	Hemp agrimony
Jacob's ladder	Hellebores	Hop
Mountain St John's wort	Sanicle	Tufted vetch
Wall lettuce	Spurge laurel	Yellow iris
Wild strawberry	White helleborine	
	Wood dog violet	
	Woodruff	
	Wood sorrel	

ACID SOILS

Heathland	Moorland	Bog
Openground		
Annual knawel	Coralwort orchid	Bogbean
Changing forget-me-not	Dwarf cornel	Bog orchid
Cudweeds	Foxgloves	Bog pondweed
Harebell	Heath bedstraw	Butterworts
Heath milkwort	Heath spotted orchid	Grass of Parnassus
Heath dog violet	Lesser butterfly orchid	Marsh asphodel
Maiden pink	Lousewort	Marsh lousewort
Petty whin	Shepherd's cress	Marsh pennywort
Sand spurrey	Sheep's sorrel	Marsh St John's wort
Spring beauty		Marsh violet
Thyme		
Tormentil		
Scrub and low bush		
Bell heather	Aspen	Bog myrtle
Bilberry	Beanberry	Bog rosemary
Broom	Crowberry	Cranberry
Downy rose	Heather	Creeping willow
Gorse	Juniper	Cross-leaved heath
Rowan		Gorse
Woodland		
Birch	Scots pine	Birch
Durmast oak		Norway spruce
Field layer		
Climbing corydalis	Bitter vetch	Chickweed
Cow wheat	Cowberry	Labrador tea
Lesser periwinkle	Creeping lady's tresses	Wintergreen
Lesser stitchwort	Twinflower	
Trailing St John's wort	Wintergreen	

NEUTRAL SOILS

Waste and rubble	Grassland	Marsh
Open ground and fields		
Broad-leaved dock	Birdsfoot trefoil	Amphibious bistort
Charlock	Common mouse-ear	Branched bur-reed
Common stitchwort	Dyer's greenweed	Broad-leaved pondweed
Common field speedwell	Great burnet	Goat willow
Dandelion	Greater butterfly orchid	Grey willow
Fumitory	Knapweed	Great willow-herb
Groundsel	Meadow buttercup	Lesser spearwort
Hoary cinquefoil	Pepper saxifrage	Marsh marigold
Poppies	Ribwort plantain	Meadowsweet
Red dead-nettle	Saw-wort	Purple loosestrife
Shepherd's purse	Yarrow	Water forget-me-nots
		Waterlilies
		Yellow iris
Scrub and low bush		
Elder	Blackthorn	Goat willow
Goat willow	Hazel	Grey willow

Waste and rubble	Grassland	Marsh
	Holly	
	Midland hawthorn	
Woodland		
Common oak	Durmast oak	Alder
	Field maple	Black poplar
	Wild service tree	Crack willow
	Wych elm	White willow
Field layer		
Barren strawberry	Anemone	Bugle
Bramble	Bugle	Creeping buttercup
Nettle	Dog violet	Creeping jenny
Rosebay willowherb	Early purple orchid	Cuckoo flower
	Hepatica	Hedge woundwort
	Primrose	Marsh thistle
	Ramsons	Ragged robin
	Red campion	Water avens
	Wolfsbane	
	Yellow pimpernel	

COASTAL VEGETATION

Saltmarsh	Dunes and sand	Rocks, cliffs, shingle
Salt air growth		
Dittander	Bloody cranesbill	Bittersweet
Grass-leaved orache	Bog pimpernel	Curled dock
Marsh mallow	Burnet rose	English stonecrop
Scurvy	Centauries	Goldilocks aster
Sea aster	Common restharrow	Goosegrass
Seablite	Creeping willow	Herb robert
Sea clover	Crow garlic	Lady's fungii
Sea lavender	Dewberry	Nottingham catchfly
Sea milkwort	Hounds tongue	Rock spurrey
Sea plantain	Marsh pennywort	Rock samphire
Sea pusslane	Purple milk-vetch	Sea campion
Sea spurrey	Ragwort	Squills
Sea wormwood	Rue-leaved saxifrage	Stocks
Wild celery	Sea bindweed	Thrift
	Sea buckthorn	Tree mallow
	Sea spurge	Wild cabbage
	Storksbill	Yellow vetch
	Wild parsley	
	Yellow-wort	
Shoreline growth		
Glasswort	Frosted orache	Oyster plant
Eelgrass	Saltwort	Sea holly
	Sea beet	Sea kale
	Sea rocket	Sea mayweed
	Sea sandwort	Sea pea
		Shrubby seablite
		Yellow horned poppy

Glossary

Acid soils: soils with a low mineral content.
Anther: part of the stamen which contains the pollen grains.
Annual: plant which lives for a year or less, completing its whole life cycle in this time. Annuals are usually shallow-rooted, and not woody.
Beak: a long projection, as in the fruits of geraniums.
Bog: wet, acid, peaty region.
Bracts: small leaf-like structures, situated beneath the flower.
Bulb: underground storage organs composed of fleshy leaves, able to remain dormant during periods unfavourable to growth.
Calyx: group of sepals, often joined together in a tube.
Casual: plant which appears irregularly.
Catkin: a hanging tassel of flowers, bunched together.
Corolla: the petals as a whole.
Deciduous: a plant which drops its leaves in autumn.
Disc florets: tube-like flowers at the centre of the flower-heads of daisies etc.
Dunes: wind-blown sand hills, usually rich in lime, interspersed with hollows called 'slacks'.
Evergreen: plant green throughout the year. Leaves are shed irregularly, not all at once.
Family: a group of plants with certain common characteristics.
Female flowers: contain styles but no stamens.
Floret: small flower, usually part of a dense cluster, as in members of the umbelliferae family.
Flower: reproductive part of a plant—usually with sepals, petals, stamens and styles.
Head: flowers crowded together at the end of a stalk.
Heath: acid-soil land, often dominated by heather.
Inflated: blown-up or bladder-like in structure; many seed pods and leaf shading have this structure.
Introduced: plants not native but brought to a place by human agency.
Leaflet: individual part of a compound leaf, such as that of ash.
Lobed: leaves very deeply toothed, but not split up into separate leaflets.
Male flower: contains fertile stamens but not styles.
Marsh: wet ground which is not peaty.
Moor: upland area, often dominated by heathers.
Native: plant occurring naturally in an area.
Naturalized: thoroughly established in an area, but originally introduced from another region.
Nectar: sugary substance, secreted by many flowers which attracts insects.
Notch: a V-shaped indentation — as in the end of a petal or leaf.
Parasite: plants which feed off other plants.
Peat: soil composed of undecayed plant matter, often acidic in character.
Perennial: plant which lives for 2 years or more, usually flowering every year. Often more robust in structure than annuals, and sometimes woody.
Pod: a simple elongated fruit, containing seeds, and splitting open when ripe.
Ray-florets: strap-shaped outer florets of many members of the daisy family.
Rhizome: creeping under-ground stem which sends up new leaves and stems each season.
Root: underground organ which absorbs water and mineral salts. (Unlike rhizomes, roots have no buds or leaf-scales.)
Rosette: flat, radiating arrangement of leaves.
Runners: creeping above-ground stems.
Sepals: ring of floral parts, ranged immediately below the petals.
Shrub: many-branched, woody plant (up to 2 metres).
Species: basic unit of classification. A group of similar individuals which interbreed.
Spike: slender, elongated cluster of flowers, usually unstalked.
Spikelet: a group of one or more grass florets.
Spur: a hollow, more or less cylindrical, projection from a petal or sepal, often containing nectar.
Stamens: male, pollen-bearing organs of a flower. Made up of stalk-like 'filament' and the pollen sac, the 'anther'. Stamens usually lie in a ring in the outer centre of the flower.
Stigma: the part of the female organ whose surface receives the pollen.
Stipules: leaf-like organs at the base of a leaf stalk, usually in pairs.
Styles: the columns of filaments, leading from the female organs (ovaries) to the stigma. They usually lie in the centre of the flower within the stamen ring.
Tendrils: twisted, thread-like appendages, part of leaf or stem, used for climbing and twining around other plants or supports.
Trefoil: with three leaflets, as in a clover leaf.
Winged: relating to stem or stalk—a flange or flanges running down a stem or stalk.

Books

FIELD GUIDES

The Wild Flowers of Britain and Northern Europe, Fitter, Fitter & Blamey, Collins, 1971, £1.60 (Paperback).

Beautifully illustrated and easy to use in the field.

Collins Pocket Guide to Wild Flowers, McClintock & Fitter, Collins, 1955, £3.

Illustrations not so fetching, but text more detailed than the previous book.

The Concise British Flora in Colour, W Keble Martin, Michael Joseph, 1965, £5·95.

Deservedly a classic. Text rather technical but illustrations a joy.

Finding Wild Flowers, R S R Fitter, Collins, £3.

A keyed identification guide linked to specific habitats with county by county run-down.

Grasses, C E Hubbard, Pelican, 1972, 60p.

Definitive grasses book. Well worth the trouble of learning how to use it.

FLOWERS OF PARTICULAR HABITATS

Wildflowers of Chalk and Limestone, J E Lousley. **Hedges,** Pollard, Hooper & Moore. **The Broads,** E A Ellis.

These and many other excellent books on specific regions and habitats are to be found in Collins New Naturalist series. Fairly advanced but very readable. Some available in Fontana paperback.

Wild Flowers, Gilmour & Walters, Collins, 1954, Fontana 1972, 60p.

Erudite and well-written survey of plants, their biology and natural habitats.

Jarrold Nature Series: Wild Flowers of the Hedgerows, Woodlands, Coast etc. All by E A Ellis, Jarrold, 40p each.

Small books of colour photographs. Short but widely informative by a man who obviously knows and loves his subject. Excellent value.

ART, FLOWER LORE, NAMES

The Englishman's Flora, Geoffrey Grigson, Paladin, 1975, £2.75.

Rich collection of common names, sayings, literary references and historical fact.

A Gardener's Dictionary of Plant Names, W T Stearn, Cassell, 1972, £3.25.

6000 latin names and their meanings, cross referenced with common names.

The Art of Botanical Illustrations, Wilfrid Blunt, Collins, £5.

A thorough study from earliest times, profusely illustrated.

MISCELLANEOUS

Everyman's Nature Reserve: Ideas for Action, ed. Eve Dennis, David and Charles, 1972, £4.95.

A collection of essays; packed with useful ideas and references.

Bellamy on Botany, 1972, **Bellamy's Britain, Bellamy's Europe,** 1976. All BBC publications, under £2.

Bellamy must be the liveliest writer on botany: all of these books are compelling reading.

A Botanist's Garden, John Raven, Collins, 1971, £2.50.

Family by family account of plants the author selected for his two gardens. European and non-European species included.

Organiza tions

Botanical Society of the British Isles (BSBI), c/o Department of Botany, British Museum (Natural History), Cromwell Road, London, SW7.

A learned botanical body. They publish the highly academic Watsonia and more readable BSBI News as well as organizing field trips all over the country.

County Naturalists Trusts

Most counties have one; they battle conservation on a local level. Particulars of individual trusts may be obtained from the **Council for Nature,** c/o The Zoo, Regent's Park, London, NW1.

Local Natural History and Botanical Societies

Much important work is done by these local groups. You should be able to get information about them from your local library, if not write to the Council for Nature for addresses.

Your wildflower garden

A number of herb farms will supply wildflower herbs by mail order. This one has a particularly good range:

Tumblers Bottom Herb Farm, Kilmersdon, Radstock,- Somerset.

Index

All English plant names are followed by their Latin counterparts; separate entries exist for plants with similar English names which belong to different Latin families.

Numbers in italics indicate illustrations.

Credits

Artists
Pat Lenander
Vanessa Luff
Ron Hayward Assoc.
John Shackell

Photographs
Heather Angel: 19, 53, 8
A-Z Collection Ltd: 36, 28, 59
Atlas Flora Europe E (Vol. 3) Helsinki: 75
Nick Birch: 45
Biophoto Assoc./Dr. Leedale: 6, 70

Marjorie Blamey: 61
Collins Pub.:74
David & Charles: 68
Ted Ellis: 12
Tony Evans: 25
Mary Evans: 56
Field Studies Council: 27
Ron & Christine Foord: 13
Fotomas Index: 46
John Freeman: 32
Sonia Halliday: 28
Hamish Hamilton: 26
Brian Hawkes: 33, 35, 93
Mansell Collection: 30
Michael Joseph: 74
Peter Myers: 59, 59

Natural History Museum: 61
NHPA/Preston Mafham: 40
Dr. Perring: 62
Radio Times Hulton Picture Lib.: 35
John & Faith Raven: 66
Tate Gallery: 44
Topham: Mick Duff: 9, 24

Cover
Design: Design Machine
Photograph: Tony Evans